1984

OUT OF THE SILENCE

Out of the Silence &

A BOOK OF FACTUAL FANTASIES

By Patrick Mahony *&&&&&&&&*

With a Foreword by Maurice Maeterlinck &

WASHINGTON, D.C.   THE INSTITUTE FOR THE STUDY OF MAN

ISBN 0-941694-17-8

First Edition, 1948
First *Institute for the Study of Man* Edition, 1984

Copyright © 1984 by Institute for the Study of Man, Inc.
1133 13th Street, N.W., Suite Comm 2
Washington, D.C. 20005

To the Memory of my Mother, Mrs. E.C. Bliss

who made all things possible

ABOUT THE AUTHOR

Patrick Mahony, the son of an Irish father and an English mother, was born in England, but educated in America. Growing up in California, the state which became his permanent home, his literary gifts led him to publish a large number of books in a variety of areas, ranging from humor and satire to travel and biography — but none were so popular as his books on the supernatural.

It is nice to know a lot — he argues — but if our beliefs and experiences were restricted to what can be explained, we would be but one tenth alive! Those who knew Patrick Mahony in life would surely confirm that beneath his urbane, assured, and courteous exterior, he fostered a deep interest in the possible survival of the human soul after death. But in his books he does not allow such convictions to take the edge off this ability to recount ghost stories with subtlety and humor. The result is a comfortable warm feeling about life — and even death — totally free from depressing fears about the world "beyond."

Most of the author's adult life was devoted to writing, lecturing, travelling, and to entertaining a wide circle of friends and acquaintances in his attractive home, nestled in a small canyon below the famous Hollywood sign which stands high in the hills above that exotic center of the imaginative and the bizarre. Conservative in his own life style, Patrick Mahony was nevertheless a talented host, and his well-known soirees attracted an ever-changing diorama of the famed and the talented. Those who were fortunate enough to be his guests will long remember his skills as a raconteur, for as Rene Fulöp-Miller expressed it: "I found that Mr. Mahony's stories held me enthralled in fascinated interest. The explanation lies in the fact that Mahony is a skilled reporter who knows a good story when he sees one, and refuses to spoil it for his readers by imposing upon them his own theoretical interpretation. I can only say that a weekend trip into Mahony's world, where three times three can be ten or eleven, is a wonderfully refreshing change from everyday life."

FOREWORD 🖂🖂🖂🖂🖂🖂🖂🖂🖂🖂🖂🖂🖂🖂🖂🖂🖂🖂

It was, I believe, the great Scottish writer, Robert Louis Stevenson, who coined the felicitous phrase of "the incommunicable thrill of things." It has application to many if not most of these stories. I felt it in reading the gem-like mystery of Rossetti's portrait of the Blessed Damozel; I felt it in reading the touching tragedy of Shanti Devi's reincarnation; and again and again I felt it as I turned over the pages of Patrick Mahony's book which is a veritable treasury of what all the opponents of crude materialism cherish as *unbelievable true stories*.

What interested me most were the phenomena emanating from beyond the grave. Such cases as are related about the work of Air Chief Marshal Lord Dowding prove that we are living in decidedly apocalyptic times. Until recently it seemed hardly possible that we would ever be able to substitute knowledge for hope and faith in human survival, but thanks to the labors of the societies for psychical research and also to the remarkable experiments of men like Dr. J. B. Rhine of Duke University, it is now a demonstrable certainty that the spiritual part of man may transcend the limits of space and time that separate us from what we call Eternity and the Beyond.

But I must not allow the prospective reader to form the impression that this is a scientific text book or that the author has some specific psychic or otherwise occult axe to grind. Patrick Mahony comes from a race of legend-minded people and hence he is a born story-teller. What he set out to do was to bring together an entertaining collection of supernormal stories. And in this he seems to have succeeded to an unusual degree.

Maurice Maeterlinck

No one who is unable to derive a sort of poetic pleasure from the fact that there are more things in heaven and earth than are dreamt of in our philosophy, should let himself be misled into reading these stories. Their chief object is entertainment, but the whole book is not only based on fact, it *is* fact, and may serve to show how wild fact can be.

Famous people figure in most of the stories because they have taken the trouble to record their experiences or because they have come under the microscope of fame. Almost all the episodes narrated involve people of high mental attributes, and what they have seen and heard with their ears and eyes they must believe to be true, no matter how fantastic it may sound to others.

This is not a book of ghost stories, although as a study of the supernormal there are several included. Personally, I have never seen a ghost, but I believe in their inherent probability. I make no claim to profound occult knowledge. I have simply collected facts—that is, what I believe any critical student would have to accept as fully authenticated facts—and these I have narrated to the best of my ability. In no case have I considered it my business to offer long-winded theoretical interpretations. The studious reader who enjoys that sort of thing may himself try his hand and mind at unriddling the phenomena presented.

There always have been people who prefer ignorance to knowledge and I expect to be attacked by skeptical readers. When I began my work on this subject, I was inclined to scoff at some of the claims made regarding psychical experiences; but I have learned to be cautious in my skepticism. And I believe that without taking the trouble of investigating the gifts of the spirit, one cannot expect to enjoy the full delights of spirituality.

My material has been drawn from many sources. I have not seen fit to burden the book with a learned bibliography but references will be found throughout the text. Acknowledgement is made with gratitude to several authors now in the Beyond whose work has been of invaluable help; also to several persons still living who have honored me with permission to use their psychical experiences. I am also indebted to Sir Hubert Wilkins and Harold Sherman for their kindness in letting me make a summary of their book, *Thoughts Through Space*. Thanks are due, too, to the editors of the magazine, *Pageant*, for allowing me to use material from a few of the stories I wrote originally for their department "World's Within." Lastly I take pleasure in recording my appreciation for the courtesy shown me by the staff of the New York Public Library and of the Library of the British Museum.

Patrick Mahony

Santa Barbara, California.

CONTENTS ♧♧♧♧♧♧♧♧♧♧♧♧♧♧♧♧♧♧♧♧♧♧

ONE

THE BORROWED BODY 𝜙𝜙𝜙𝜙𝜙𝜙𝜙𝜙𝜙𝜙𝜙𝜙

Mr. and Mrs. Thomas J. Vennum moved to Watseka, Iroquois County, Illinois, in the spring of 1875, settling down with their daughter Lurancy in a modest house on the outskirts of that town.

One hot hazy evening in July, 1877, the little girl, who was then about twelve years old, fell down on the floor in a violent cataleptic fit. A hideous scream broke from her body. Her cheeks began to tremble; her whole face became distorted; the eyebrows and the skin of the forehead contracted as in a dark frown; the eyelids quivered as all her features twisted in horrible convulsions.

When Lurancy regained consciousness her entire personality had altered. Her face, formerly characterized by a dull woodenness of expression, took on a relaxed sweetness, and her once listless eyes changed from furtive to straightforward in their glance. Her voice, which had been monotonous and colorless, developed a warm richness of tone.

3

But, most staggering of all the things arising from her fit, Lurancy regarded everyone, including her parents, as total strangers. Moreover, she insisted that she was not their child; she could not recall any details of her existence with them and referred to herself as Mary Roff.

Although the Vennums knew that a family by the name of Roff lived somewhere in the town, they gave this detail no significance until a specialist was called in. After deliberation he suggested that the Roffs be asked to come to see Lurancy, hoping that thus by a strange twist some light might be shed on the mystery of her condition.

In due course Mr. and Mrs. Asa Roff came to call and Lurancy flung herself into their arms with the greatest emotion, asking the most knowing personal questions about them and addressing them as Ma and Pa. Her real parents were dumbfounded, naturally enough, feeling especially hurt at the effusive affection with which she embraced the Roffs. As their child she had been incapable of sentiment and quite undemonstrative.

Then it was that the Roffs revealed the amazing fact that they had once had a daughter named Mary who had died about twelve years previously, the exact year in which Lurancy was born. The child was very delicate, and for the first years of her life the family traveled in search of the proper climate for her health. A disease of the lungs, aggravated by cataleptic fits, eventually carried her off. Ever since the tragedy of· her death the Roffs had been making efforts to communicate with her by spiritualism, and they now regarded the obsession of Lurancy Vennum as the realization of their dreams. Their daughter had been re-

4

born, and they claimed that the two personalities coincided exactly.

The Vennums faced a *fait accompli*. Their daughter's personality was now controlled by another, and on their physician's advice they yielded to the pleadings of the Roffs that she be allowed to go and reside for the time being with them. Not only would it be a pleasant home for her, but it would mean the utmost bliss for the formerly bereaved parents of Mary.

Not a day went by without their reborn child mentioning to Asa and his wife little events that had occurred during her first existence on this planet. Referring to her early childhood and the time when she had once been taken to Texas, she said one day: "Do you remember us crossing the Red River and seeing all those Indians? What's happened to Mrs. Reeder's girls who lived next door to us then, I wonder?" On another occasion she picked out accurately the place where she had buried her pet dog before she died in Watseka.

Most curious of all was her absolute ignorance of time, which she seemed unable to compute. A day, a week, a month were almost the same thing to her. She did not seem aware of her own age. In identifying articles of clothing belonging to her as Mary she would say: "Oh, there's a headdress I wore a long time ago." Or: "I must wear that again soon before it gets too old." When she met an old friend, whom the family had known in Texas and who was married to a man named Lord, she remarked: "You know, Mrs. Lord, you look so natural and have changed the least of any since I came back."

In her previous body she had been born on October 8, 1846, and her sister Minerva, the Roffs' older child, was born two years earlier. On hearing the strange news, she lost no time in going to Watseka. Without being told who the visitor was, the child caught her round the neck, crying for joy. "Nervie, oh Nervie," she exclaimed happily, "will you play those hopping games we used to do?" Thus she addressed her "sister" by the nickname the family had used when both girls were children together.

Many other details came out which she could not possibly have learned from outsiders. Daguerreotypes of Mary and Lurancy exist which bear concrete evidence of the physical resemblance of the two girls. All who had known Mary declared that their personalities were similar in every way also. At the time of the peak in his happiness, Mr. Roff wrote to Mr. Vennum: "The dear angel recognizes everybody and everything Mary knew before she died. If anything should happen to her we should both be inconsolable."

Mary apparently realized that she had control of Lurancy's body only for a certain length of time. One day she said: "I must kiss you often, Ma and Pa, while I have lips to kiss you with and arms to hug you with. But when I go back I shall still be in touch with you, as before."

On May 7, the following year, the child was found crying. Tears cascaded down her face as she told the Roffs that the time had come for Lurancy to return to her own body. She pressed them to her breast and slowly proceeded to go into a cataleptic state. A doctor was called, and he declared that the delirium was something quite alien to common catalepsy, but that the state of unconsciousness would not last long.

In about an hour the change had taken place. Lurancy was in control of her body once more. Quite dazed, she asked in a voice unknown to the Roffs: "Where am I? Where have I been? I was never here before."

The only possible course was for her to be returned to her original parents, and, heartbroken, Mr. and Mrs. Roff went into mourning a second time. In 1887, Lurancy married a farmer named George Binning and died at the age of fifty-five in 1920. As far as is known she experienced no further spirit invasions.

THE ETHERIC DOUBLE 🐦🐦🐦🐦🐦🐦🐦🐦🐦🐦🐦

Until the Russians took over Latvia, there flourished in the small town of Valmiera, some fifty miles from Riga, a fashionable girls' finishing school, the "Pensionat Neuwelcke."

Many years ago a French teacher named Mlle Émélie Sagée, born in Dijon, lived in the school. She was a model of a governess: exacting and firm, yet patient and popular with the students. About thirty-five years old, she liked her position and the directors were most satisfied with her.

After she had been there a few months, however, rumors

began to spring up about her. One student would report having seen her in a certain room, while another insisted that she had just run into her in some corridor at the other end of the building.

For a time this passed as a joke, but as it recurred again and again it came to be considered rather odd.

One day, while holding class, Mlle Sagée was illustrating the lesson on the blackboard with a class of twelve girls watching her. To their utter consternation they all suddenly beheld two Mlle Sagées: one by the side of the other, exactly alike. They used the same gestures, only one could be seen writing with a piece of chalk while the double was merely imitating her.

At another time, a class of embroidery was being held in the Assembly Room, a spacious hall with four large French windows. The students were seated in such a way that they could see out into the garden where Mlle Sagée was gathering flowers. The presiding mistress got up from the large armchair in which she was seated to leave the room for a few minutes. Then, of a sudden, there appeared seated in the same chair the figure of the French teacher. Looking into the garden, the students could see that she was still in reality picking flowers outside but doing so now in a quite indifferent, perfunctory manner. It was as though a rigid apathy had crept over her, and her activity was a great effort.

Yet there, as large as life, she also sat before the class, without moving, palpably human. One of the girls later related how she had gone up and touched the figure which did not stir and had a soft feel like cotton-wool. As soon as the mistress returned, the figure disappeared, and it was observed that Mlle Sagée's flower-picking took on a more vigorous air.

Prior to this the directors had heard some rumors but felt the matter too ridiculous to warrant serious investigation. With these two overt instances, however, the whole matter came under their earnest scrutiny. To make things worse, one of the girls had written home about it, and the parents registered a complaint.

Under cross-examination Mlle Sagée was diffident at first. On being told that the incidents had assumed proportions that would require her resignation, she completely broke down. "It is very, very hard, Mesdames," she sobbed, addressing the three directors. "This is the tenth time I have had to leave a position for the same reason." She went on to explain that although she was able to project her astral double at will, she had no power to repress it. She had tried her best to keep it under control, but it would come in veritable epidemics. Sometimes she would go for a year without one of the appearances; and then again they would come in a series, in various degrees of density.

The directors were sympathetic, and it was agreed that she would leave with a certain stipend. All the girls were downcast at the news and insisted on giving her a party.

At the dinner in her honor, standing beside her and imitating every eating function, appeared her etheric counterpart, a scene which was witnessed this time by the entire school. And when she rose from her chair, the double took the seat, remaining there until after she had left the room.

What became of Émélie Sagée is not known, except that

for a time she went to live with a relative in Dijon who had two young children. They often told their mother that they had seen two Aunt Émélies, but they did not complain and seemed to love them both equally well.

SELF-PORTRAIT FROM THE PAST ⚘⚘⚘⚘⚘

Dante Gabriel Rossetti, poet and leader of the Pre-Raphaelite Brotherhood of art in nineteenth-century England, possessed the imaginative spirit to a rare degree, especially in his paintings, which are pervaded with mysticism. In part this is due to the unusual model who posed for many of them and whose significance and influence continued long after her death.

In 1848, a friend of the artist discovered working in a modiste's shop Elizabeth Siddall who had, as Swinburne said, "matchless loveliness, courage, endurance, humor, sweetness, too dear to be profaned by any attempt of expression."

In the process of painting her, Rossetti fell madly in love with her and his love was as madly returned. As he sketched the delicate refinements of the lovely face, her features became enshrined in his heart. Never was there a more poetic resemblance between an idea and a face, and possibly some of the charm which enabled him to confer on her such immortality was owing to the frequent shadow of a resigned sadness which fell often, like a veil, over her sweet face. Her personality exhaled the tragic radiance of someone not long for this world.

Tuberculosis finally laid its terrible hands on Elizabeth, and Rossetti was told the brutal truth that his beloved would soon fade away and die. He married her at once, vowing that he would nurse her back to health. But she passed away and he sorrowed unspeakably. He gathered up all the poems he had written to her and while her coffin lay open, laid them between her cheek and the folds of her hair. No gesture of mourning could have been more touching and appropriate, for her value to him was evident in all his work not only during the time he had known her, but forever after.

The rest of his life remained dedicated to the last and most stirring passion of his existence. He traced those misty features of Elizabeth in all his paintings and left a fitting tribute to her in the *Beata Beatrix*, the most famous of all his paintings.

At the public showing of this masterpiece, critics acclaimed it as his finest work, one of them commenting casually that there was a curious resemblance between it and the painting of St. Agnes of the Intercession which he had seen in a museum at Bologna in Italy. He assumed that Mr. Rossetti had seen it too and suggested that it had to be considered the inspiration of the *Beata Beatrix*.

Rossetti, however, had never been to Italy, nor had he seen a reproduction of the painting in question. He made inquiries and found that it was done by an artist named Angiolieri who had lived four hundred years ago.

A haunting desire to see the portrait took possession of

him. But his health was now failing and he could not undertake so long a journey. Some years after Elizabeth's death, however, Dante Gabriel's brother, William Michael Rossetti, had to go to Italy and agreed to stop over at Bologna and try to look into the matter.

Not without difficulty William Michael located the gallery wherein hung the portrait of St. Agnes. Though her hands were not joined as in his brother's work and her face was slightly forward, not upturned, this St. Agnes looked exactly like the model of the *Beata Beatrix* that had been painted in London four hundred years later. The mouth had the same supremely gentle expression, and the eyes reflected the same dreamlike inwardness.

Thrilled almost to the point of tears, William Michael Rossetti looked through the catalogue to see if there might be something about the model whom Angiolieri had used for his portrait of St. Agnes, but there was only a reference to Angiolieri himself. At another wing of the same gallery a self-portrait of his was to be found.

A quiet uncertain fear came over Rossetti as a guide showed him the way. Darkness had fallen when he reached the spot where the picture was hanging. The old attendant held the lamp up to it, and by its flickering light he saw a grave, black-bearded person, the very image of his brother.

Back in London he told his ailing brother of his discovery. Was it possible that Dante Gabriel Rossetti himself had lived the life of the Italian painter and that his beloved wife had posed for the portrait of St. Agnes?

As though in anticipation of this experience he had written in his poem "Sudden Light:"

I have been here before,
But when or how I cannot tell:
I know the grass beyond the door,
The sweet keen smell,
The sighing sound, the lights around the shore.

SUTTEE IN SWITZERLAND 🔔🔔🔔🔔🔔🔔🔔🔔

There died some years ago in an insane asylum on the shores of Lake Léman in Switzerland a woman whose story has gone into the annals of psychiatry as an extreme instance of the most peculiar form of somnambulism. Professor Flournoy, sometime Professor of Psychology at Geneva University, spent years observing the extraordinary phases of the nocturnal trances of Mlle Hélène Smith, as he calls her in a scholarly study devoted to the case.

When the phenomenon first occurred, she was a young woman in her teens. She had had no artistic education, but in her somnambulistic behavior she displayed the ability to enact scenes which were totally unrelated to her waking life with such perfection, originality and grace as the most accomplished actress could not have surpassed after months of study.

Her parents would not have worried too much if their daughter had simply walked about the house in her sleep, as

13

sensitive young people are often known to do, especially during the difficult period of adolescence; but when they observed that Hélène was acting out very dramatic and realistic scenes, they were terribly frightened. Their doctor, however, bade them calm their fears, explaining that the young woman was merely expressing a theme that was the product of her subliminal self (whatever that may mean).

It was not until Professor Flournoy interested himself in the case that the very strange peculiarities which characterized it came to light. It was quite obvious that in her somnambulistic fits Hélène was re-enacting scenes from a very distant past, either as though she were repeating experiences she herself had had in an earlier incarnation or as though a spirit from the past were temporarily crowding out her normal ego.

Entering into the middle of the moon-lit floor of the drawing room in her home, Hélène came forward with eyes strained and hands outstretched. With consummate artistry she expressed her predicament so graphically that the professor and her parents knew that she was about to undergo a great ordeal. Flournoy was quick to grasp the significance as she walked several times round an imaginary object, making reverential gestures. "It is a funeral pyre," he whispered. "She is going to throw herself onto the flames as an act of devotion to her dead husband." She was, in fact, enacting a ceremony in which Hindu widows used to burn themselves with their husband's body in order to enjoy happiness in heaven.

Solemnly she addressed someone who must have been her

son: "Take this poniard which my husband employed over his enemies. Never use it for any other purpose. Govern your subjects like a father, as he did, and your life will be long and happy. Since he is gone, there is nothing to detain me here, and all I can do is to follow him."

Then, turning towards the flaming pyre and pronouncing the names of her gods, she threw herself upon it, uttering the most piercing screams.

A striking fact about Hélène's nocturnal performances was that they seemed to follow the inverted order of historical chronology. This, Professor Flournoy soon recognized, was quite in keeping with the theory that memories of a past existence revert first to the more recent occurrences and only later to the more remote. On this basis it became possible to piece together a story of Hélène's previous Hindu existence, or, if one prefers, of the earthly life of the spirit invading her in her somnambulistic trances. She had been the daughter of a wealthy Arab sheik, living at the close of the Fourteenth Century, and at about eighteen she had become the wife of a Hindu potentate.

As the Princess Simandini she was passionately devoted to her husband Sivrouka Nayaka, who reigned over the fortress Tchandraguiri. He died in 1401, and his widow elected to become a suttee, that is, she insisted on being burned alive at his funeral.

Professor Flournoy spared no effort in consulting all the eminent historians and orientalists to obtain confirmation of these references, but not one of them was able to furnish him with the slightest clew. All the names Hélène had uttered were totally unknown to them; they could not recall any, real or fictitious, that in any way resembled them.

The tenacious psychologist, however, persisted until he found what he was seeking. In an ancient tome by a long unread author named De Marles, a copy of which he had located at the Library of the British Museum, he accidentally came across the following: "Kanara and neighboring provinces on the side towards Delhi may be regarded as the Georgia of Hindustan . . . Tchandraguiri, which signifies Mountain of the Moon, is a vast fortress constructed by Rajah Sivrouka, who died in 1401."

The copy of the De Marles book at the British Museum is one of very few in existence. There is none in Geneva, so that Hélène could not possibly have read it.

After a while Hélène began enacting scenes from other previous lives with equal perfection. The Hindu cycle had continued for almost a year when one night Flournoy noticed that she had taken on the characteristics of a less exotic personality. Humility and orientalism were exchanged for tragic grace and elegance combined with grim horror, as Hélène acted out a scene on the guillotine which was unmistakably the execution of Marie Antoinette.

Students of the unhappy queen's life were invited to witness subsequent performances which were located in the gardens and apartments of the Petit Trianon. Kneeling before the cradle of the baby Dauphin she would sing in a foreign voice and accent nursery rhymes actually composed by Marie Antoinette herself.

But the most amazing thing to happen was that she signed her name to a formal edict to the Court. It was found that

16

the signature was absolutely identical with that of the famous queen.

After five years of observation and study, Professor Flournoy came to the conclusion that the trances of Hélène Smith could only be explained by the assumption that discarnate powers were responsible for them. However that may be, the effect on her nervous system was more than it could bear and she finally lost her reason.

RESCUE AT SEA 🎕🎕🎕🎕🎕🎕🎕🎕🎕🎕🎕🎕🎕🎕🎕

The first mate of the S.S. Vestris, bound for St. Johns, New Brunswick, in 1828, was young Robert Bruce, a direct collateral descendant of the Liberator of Scotland.

One day at noon he was on deck with the captain taking an observation of the sun. Afterwards both went below for the purpose of calculating the day's run.

The mate struggled with his calculations for some time, and as they did not seem to come out accurately, he finally went into the captain's cabin. "Sorry, Sir. I can't make it come out right," he said.

Slowly the man seated at the desk turned his head toward him; he seemed to answer, but said nothing. As the light struck the man's features, Bruce felt an electric shock go through him. It was not the captain he saw, but a complete stranger who resembled no one else on board. He met the man's fixed gaze in frightened silence, then ran out of the cabin and up the gangway trembling all over.

Up on deck he found the captain. "Sir, there's a stranger in your cabin," he cried breathlessly.

"A stranger? You must be mad. It must have been the steward or the second mate. Who else would dare enter my cabin without my orders?"

"No, Sir," insisted Bruce, "it was a face I have never seen before in my life."

"Go below again and take another look," bellowed the captain.

"I am no coward, Sir, as you know, but if it's what I think it is down there, I'd rather not go alone."

The captain pooh-poohed the whole affair but agreed to go with him. They found nobody in the cabin. The ship was immediately searched, and no unknown person was on board. Bruce became the laughingstock of the whole ship.

"If I didn't see that man writing on your slate, Sir, I'll give up a whole year's pay!" he said stubbornly.

"Ah, then the writing should still be there. Show me that slate."

The slate was still on the desk, and in a moment it was in the captain's hands. Sure enough, there was some writing on it!

"This must be your handwriting, Bruce," said the captain holding up the slate, on which was written in legible letters: *Steer North West!* "Come now, are you playing a schoolboy's trick on me? Let's see you write down those words."

Bruce's handwriting was compared with that on the slate, but it was not at all like it. Then all the members of the crew who could write were made to furnish specimens of their hand. But the handwriting was in no case similar. Finally the captain went into a brown study, pondering the mysterious happening.

"I am a God-fearing man," he said at length. "There must be some hidden meaning to the message, some providential force at work. We'll steer North West for a while and see what happens."

The order was obeyed. In a little while, an iceberg was reported ahead. When the ship neared, it was seen in the twilight that there was another vessel there, wrecked and frozen to the ice, its decks swept by lashing waves. The Vestris hove to and found a number of survivors. The wreck had already been there for some days, they learned. The rescue came just in time, for their provisions and water were almost gone, and the men were sick and cold.

As one by one the shipwrecked mariners were brought on board to safety, Bruce suddenly noticed one in particular. It was the very image of the man he had seen writing on the slate. The man returned his look with the same fixed stare as before.

As soon as the rescue was completed, Bruce told the captain of his discovery. Then together they talked to the captain of the wreck. "Yes, I know what you mean," he said slowly. "He predicted that we would be rescued on this very day."

The man was called into the cabin. He told them that a few hours before the rescue, that is to say, at about the time when the weird apparition was seen by the mate, he had been sleeping heavily. He had dreamed that he was on board another ship and that they were coming to rescue the ship on the ice. Moreover, he recognized in detail the Vestris as the ship he had seen in his dream.

Stupefied, the captain picked up the slate on which still appeared the uncanny message. "Copy that down," he commanded. The dazed seaman copied: "Steer North West." And the handwriting of the two messages was the same.

PRINCESS CARABOO ᪥᪥᪥᪥᪥᪥᪥᪥᪥᪥᪥᪥᪥᪥

The shades of evening were about to close on a dull, cold, rainy day early in April, 1817, in the village of Almondsbury, in Somerset, England, when an exquisite young woman appeared at the Inn dressed in clothes the style of which was of another age or place. She was about seventeen years old, not quite five feet tall. A fine head was framed by long blonde hair which she wore in plaits; a pretty nose above a perfect mouth; and eyes like pools of sea-water.

She was apparently unable to speak English and tried to make clear by signs that she required lodging for the night. The proprietor was just about going to send her away, thinking her to be a vagrant, when the local magistrate happened to pass by. He was a kindly man who was quite touched by her sad plight, and questioned her in a very fatherly way. To his patiently repeated "Who are you?" she finally answered: "Caraboo, Caraboo." And so the judge laughingly named her Princess Caraboo because of the similarity of the name to that of the fairy princess in Cinderella who drives about in her coach drawn by rats and mice.

Princess Caraboo was taken to live with Judge and Mrs. Worrall at their country mansion. There the strange young woman stayed for some time and no effort was spared to solve the mystery of her origin. A sample record of her speech taken down by Mrs. Worrall shows how difficult this must have been. "Te rumete tau. Illee lete luto scele. Impe re scele lee luto. Onko keere scete tere lute. Ombo lute sinte imbo."

At first it was thought she was speaking some patois of Javanese, but after a student of that language had examined her, this theory had to be abandoned, and her language has remained a complete and utter mystery. This, however, did not prevent her from insinuating herself into the good graces of the Worralls and their coterie of friends. She managed to learn a few words of English but never became articulate enough to explain her background. Every day she exercised with a stick as a sword and she showed great prowess in handling a bow and arrow.

The London *Times* covered the odd facts of her story, and in a little while she was nationally famous. She was lionized in Bristol, being entertained by certain titled people of the time.

Later an American circus owner engaged her at a good fee to appear as a side show, and she took ship for the States in September, 1817. Here her name became linked with that of a rich man with whom a marriage was finally arranged. But on the eve of the wedding she disappeared, leaving no trace behind her.

REBORN TO DIE &&&&&&&&&&&&&&&

Shanti Devi, a little Hindu girl with a pinched face and a woebegone expression, was born on October 12, 1926. She grew into a child contemplative and dreamy, not caring to play with other children.

Her parents became alarmed about her when she began saying things which touched upon the recollections of a previous existence, for it is a Hindu tradition that a child disclosing knowledge of a past life will die young.

At first Shanti's parents paid no attention to such remarks as: "My husband in Muttra always preferred me to wear this color," or: "I'd like to give this to my dear little son." But when she began giving details of her previous existence in Muttra, a town many miles distant from Delhi, they went to consult the local schoolmaster.

To their astonishment, he explained that he had always been under the impression that she actually came from Muttra because she spoke with a marked accent of that district. He suggested that they quiz Shanti seriously in an effort to shed light on the riddle.

The schoolmaster himself asked her point blank about

this "husband," and, just as all Hindu women are reluctant to sound the name of their spouse, Shanti had to be coaxed to give it. Finally she uttered the name of Kedar Nath Chaubey.

The strange story of Shanti Devi came to the attention of Lala Deschbandu Gupta, a close associate of the Mahatma Gandhi. Through him it was established that there was actually living at Muttra a man by the name of Keda Nath Chaubey who had been widowed sometime before the birth of Shanti Devi.

When the child was taken to Muttra to verify some of her statements, she was able to show the party the way to Mr. Chaubey's house. She described roads and streets leading to it before they got there, also the Temple of Dwarkashish, at which she remembered worshiping, all with the minutest accuracy. In an offhand way she would refer to little things which could only be known to someone thoroughly familiar with the district.

Confronted with Kedar Nath Chaubey, she immediately recognized him as her husband, giving convincing answers to the most personal questions concerning their former life together. Mr. Chaubey's wife had died on October 4, 1925 of childbirth complications, leaving him a son born on September 25. He was a merchant engaged in the cloth business.

Mr. Chaubey declared that listening to Shanti was just like listening to his deceased wife, so close was the resemblance in their mannerisms and speech. After a little while both man and child were moved to the point of tears. In her former life Shanti Devi had been born in September, 1902.

Even more touching was the scene when Shanti met her

"son." The five-year-old girl reacted in the most maternal way to the little boy one year her elder. At once a bond sprang up between the children. No one could doubt that they were the same soul; she pressed him to her heart as if she would never let him go.

Later she identified out of a crowd of people her former mother and father who wept with the greatest emotion on embracing their daughter. She recognized her brother, now twenty-five years old.

So perfectly did she remember her earlier life that she was able to discover some jewels which she had hidden before she died and which had been the object of a vain search by her husband after her death.

Her attachment for her "son" was something that could not be treated lightly. With the assent of Mr. Chaubey, it was decided that the children should be allowed to remain together, and Shanti's family took both of them back to Delhi.

In the end the Hindu legend had its way. Both "mother" and "son" died within a few months of each other in the year 1939; she was twelve and he had just turned thirteen.

STEVE DONOGHUE AND BROWN JACK

Not long before Steve Donoghue died, in the halcyon days of 1939, a dinner was given him by some of his fellow jockeys. The speeches were broadcast, and a loud-speaker was fitted up in the stable of Steve's favorite horse Brown Jack, many miles away at Thorpe Lubenham in Hertfordshire.

Steve addressed a few words to the former darling of the tracks. "I am thinking of you, Brown Jack, and I hope your ears are burning," he said. At once Brown Jack's ears went up. He knew that voice well, and he listened attentively as it whispered: "Good night, Brown Jack, I'll be seeing you."

When the great jockey lay dying some time later, Brown Jack went off his food and lost several pounds, so close was the communion between man and animal.

No other horse in modern times has so belied his capacity by his appearance. Brown Jack's knobbly knees and bad proportions made him look like a giant rocking horse. When his owner took him to England from his native Eire, he was tried out for flat racing. Several of the jockeys that rode him were ashamed of his awkward gait, and one of them actually refused to mount him.

It was not until Steve Donoghue ran across Brown Jack that his amazing success on the turf began. Their first race together was the Alexander Stakes at Ascot, the longest race on the calendar, which Jack and Steve won by four lengths, the first of seven winnings by them of this race alone!

Donoghue was quick to recognize the remarkable powers of the Irish stayer who took to racing like an infant does to milk. It soon became evident that the horse knew many invaluable tricks and secrets about his art which he had had no chance to learn by experience, and many experts in horse-flesh were convinced that Brown Jack was a case of equine

25

reincarnation. A case in point was the way in which he would conserve his energies for a final spurt as soon as he heard the roar of the crowd. Nothing ever seemed to worry him; he never became excited or on his toes. "He has done it all before in a previous life," said Steve after their first victory together. "I am as sure of that as I am of my own pre-existence."

Then, one day, an amazing thing happened. Steve was visiting the horse prior to a new race and Jack kept on scraping his right hoof on the stable floor as if he were trying to write. Having heard of the talking horses of Elberfeld, Donoghue, just for a lark, told the groom to prepare some die on the ground outside on which they marked out the various letters of the alphabet.

When Jack was taken there, he shied a little but then proceeded to spell out one or two three-letter words, choosing the characters with his right hoof. The first word was "we," after which he spelled "won" afterwards correcting it to "win."—In this he was correct because he and his rider actually won the race that took place that day. For some reason Steve was substituted at the last minute and the chances for a victory were rather in doubt.

In the period of his smashing performances, Jack would usually run his own show, so to speak. His idiosyncrasies were many. One of them was that he disliked having his box cleaned out too often, expressing his displeasure in no uncertain way when it was. He would not sleep like other horses but took his rest with his forelegs cocked slightly in the air. This worried his trainer who feared that it would mark his coat and make him still more ridiculous. So a piece of felt was nailed where the wood might harm him, but Jack objected and tore it off over and over again until he got his way.

Steve rode him to victory in over thirty races. In the Roseberry Memorial Stakes in 1930, they beat the entry of King George the Fifth. Afterwards His Majesty said to Steve: "I never mind being beaten by a horse like Brown Jack." And Steve replied: "You see, Sir, he has passed this way before."

TWO

A MESSAGE OF HOPE ಕಾಕಾಕಾಕಾಕಾಕಾಕಾಕಾಕಾಕಾಕಾ

About eight o'clock on a brisk October evening in 1944, a knock came on the door of the home of Dr. and Mrs. William Spickers at Franklin Lakes, New Jersey.

Mrs. Spickers went to answer it but did so a little hesitatingly and with a strange foreboding. Silhouetted in the doorway was the figure of a tall stranger dressed rather like a country parson.

"I am looking for the house of Mr. and Mrs. Jones, and I seem to be lost," he said in a kindly voice. "Perhaps you can direct me."

There happened to be no one by that name living in the neighborhood, and Mrs. Spickers asked the stranger to come inside thinking she could make some inquiries for him.

The man seemed to grow in stature when he came into the full light of the living room. His whole appearance reminded his hosts most strikingly of Abraham Lincoln. A hint of grey in his dark hair set off his finely chiseled features, and some high-minded lines about the mouth gave the finishing touch to an impressive personality. Ingenuous eyes focused on the doctor and his wife as they suggested he sit down while Mrs. Spickers did some telephoning.

Dr. Spickers got into conversation with the stranger, who explained that the people he sought had lost their son in the war. This led to the topic of how differently people take the assaults of sorrow, how varied are their reactions. Later on the doctor recalled with amazement the quick rapport which had been established between him and the visitor. It was as if they had known each other a long time.

After Mrs. Spickers returned from an unsuccessful attempt to locate the Jones family, she joined the two men in their conversation which continued for another half hour or so. Everything the unknown man said was marked by profound beauty of thought and diction.

"That we must lose in the flesh in order to possess spiritual values is a grievous truth established by a thousand facts," he observed. "I always remember the words of Emerson after his grief over the death of the woman he loved: 'When the half-gods go, the Gods arrive.' It should never be forgotten that tears are merely the dew which falls on the flower we call Hope. At last, with this grim war, people can see again the everlasting things that matter, some of which they had forgotten."

As he recited these fine reflections, Dr. and Mrs. Spickers recall that his whole being lit up in an effulgent light. "Those are wonderful words," the doctor said, "I cannot help thinking that Lincoln might have said something like that." And then he added: "As a physician I know that every onslaught in human life must be fought out on the battleground of the mind."

A smile was painted on the stranger's face. Kindheartedly and very loftily he replied: "Remember that a life gone from sight and hearing is not necessarily lost. Among the mystic qualities of the soul, memory is the most precious of all. That is my parting message to you and many other parents of fine sons in the war."

Startled Dr. and Mrs. Spickers exclaimed: "How did you know we have a son in the war?"

The stranger assumed an air of great dignity as he made ready to go. "You see, I know a great many of them." Then he was gone.

That same night word came by telegram from the War Department that Lieutenant Albert Spickers had been killed in a crash of a bomber plane.

POSTHUMOUS PAINTING 🖋🖋🖋🖋🖋🖋🖋🖋🖋🖋

Robert Swain Gifford was an American scenic artist of some note who died in 1905. Many of his landscapes hang in museums throughout America and represent the artist's love of New England. A posthumous exhibit was held in the latter part of January 1906, at the American Art Galleries in New York City. A certain Mr. J. L. Thompson who was a goldsmith, went to see the exhibit because he remembered having sold Mr. Gifford some jewelry years before and somehow he was interested in his late client's talent.

While looking admiringly at the paintings a voice came into his ears repeating like a gramophone record: "You see what I have done . . . You must take up and finish my work . . . You see what I have done . . . You must take up and finish my work . . ." There followed strange visions of twisted old trees whose leaves appeared to tremble with secret horror, set against a storm-wracked sky. The pale orb of the moon emitted luminous streams of light on two black windmills in the distance, one with gigantic motionless sails and the other wingless, and both of them almost eclipsed by the gnarled trees. Mr. Thompson was unable to understand the meaning of these visions although he realized that they had deep allegorical significance, giving the impression of a human being in haste and panic.

Mr. Thompson became so conscious of all this that he could not go on with his work. The voice and the visions cast a cloud over his whole life. Finally his wife took him to see a psychiatrist who recommended that he be sent to an institution.

In some way his case came to the attention of Professor James H. Hyslop, a psychologist and specialist in cases of obsession. Dr. Hyslop suggested that Mr. Thompson try to paint the scenes which haunted him hoping through that medium to unpack the patient's mind. Before this time the goldsmith had done some occasional sketching which he had learned in a very elementary art course.

As soon as he put his visions on to canvas his health improved and strangely enough, the paintings proved of such merit that he was advised to show them to the art critic James B. Townsend. This gentleman was so struck by their quality that he bought one at once, and without knowing any of the odd facts that inspired their creator, he remarked that the style reminded him very much of the late Robert Swain Gifford.

Encouraged by the monetary gain but still haunted by the visions of the trees, the budding artist set out in a resolve to verify his apparitions. This he thought would be possible by a trip to Nonquitt, Massachusetts, the summer home of Gifford. He actually went there in July, 1907, and the first thing he did was to call on Mrs. Gifford.

When he had explained the reason for his call, the widow took him into the studio of her husband which had not been used since the artist's death. In a frenzy of surprise Thompson saw on the easel an unfinished painting of trees absolutely identical with those of his vision which he had painted some months before.

Mr. Thompson then went to the island where Mrs. Gifford stated her husband had been painting in the autumn before he died and where a severe storm had interrupted his work the last time he was there.

Wandering about for a half hour or so the visitor came upon the scene of his hallucination. Here were the hoary trees, twisted in horrible convulsions, and in the distance the two mills. Out came his sketch book and just as he put pencil to paper the voice resounded in his ear: "Go and look on the other side of the furthest tree." And on the opposite side of the tree he found the initials "R.S.G. 1902" carved on the bark.

All these facts were verified by Dr. Hyslop who states in his book, *Contact with the Other World*, that the initials were aged by several years and could not possibly have been carved by Mr. Thompson. The original paintings by Mr. Gifford and the ones of Mr. Thompson's vision, together with photographs of the scenes are on view at the American Society for Psychical Research in New York City.

A GIFT FROM THE GRAVE ᕯᕯᕯᕯᕯᕯᕯᕯ

The name of Mrs. Patrick Campbell is still apt to arouse varying emotions and reminiscences in those that knew her in person or remember having seen her on the stage. To her intimate friends she was a lovable woman whose very faults could but add to her fascination. At times, it is true, she was mean and vindictive, and especially towards the end of her career she would often fall back on inflicting petty humiliations on those around her. The treatment she meted out to many who tried to help her inspired the witty remark of Alexander Woollcott that she was "a sinking ship firing on her rescuers."

Some years before she died she fell seriously ill in her London home and was befriended by Sara Allgood, the Irish Bernhardt who became later a feature player in the films of Hollywood. "I see myself already in the tomb," Mrs. Campbell said when she thought her life was ebbing.

"I had hoped to get far away from here to die, to a place where I would not be known. There is a certain charm in being forgotten after a life spent before the public."

But the great actress rallied. She, who for years had filled the theatrical world with admiration for the power of her genius and fear of the biting sarcasm of her wry wit, now went to France, sad and broken-hearted and with but one thought: to die in peace. Before leaving she expressed her gratitude to Miss Allgood by giving her a few personal mementos, a teapot and a framed water color of a heron.

Not long afterwards Sara Allgood was called to Hollywood to make a moving picture, the result of which was a long-term contract. She bought herself a home, and the teapot Mrs. Campbell had given her was soon in use and the picture of the heron adorned a wall in her boudoir.

Being Irish, Sara Allgood believes that the first dream one has in a new home comes true. The peculiar thing about this particular dream was that every detail of it had the same exaggerated clearness as is characteristic of stereoscopic vision. On the horizon there appeared, as though by magic, a locomotive which whistled by at full speed. Everything was in its logical place as in a real view, but the absolutely distinctive feature was the emotion aroused when the train came to an abrupt halt some distance after it had passed the station. Mrs. Campbell alighted and came running up to her old friend. She was looking pale and wan, as though she had been undergoing a great strain.

Before Sara could express her astonishment, Mrs. Campbell held a hushed finger to her lips: "Have you found my gift from the grave? Look behind the picture." These words were uttered with that sublime air of boredom which had been one of her admired feats on the stage.

The dream came as a surprise to Sara Allgood, for although she knew that her friend was then at Pau in Southern France, living there under Nazi occupation, a report had come through that Mrs. Campbell was safe and well. Next morning Miss Allgood immediately went to the wall and took down the picture of the heron, and removing the backboard, she found a caricature of the actress done by Max Beerbohm and signed by him. It was a gift worth something in excess of a thousand dollars.

In the evening papers a release from Pau announced that Mrs. Campbell had died in the previous night.

LOLA MONTEZ 💞💞💞💞💞💞💞💞💞💞💞💞💞💞💞💞

In 1929, Rudi Schneider, reputed to be the world's greatest physical medium, was brought to England by Dr. Harry Price, head of the National Laboratory of Psychical Research. The supernormal gifts of this young Austrian, who was a motor mechanic by trade, had been tested in various Continental cities, and no trickery has ever been recorded against him.

Dr. Price is a very skeptical investigator, and although he

was deeply impressed with what he had seen of Rudi's performances abroad, he was anxious to test him under the absolutely fraud-proof conditions of his own laboratory.

One of the remarkable things about the mediumship of Rudi Schneider was that his trance personality was a woman who said she was Lola Montez, the famed mistress of King Louis I of Bavaria. But more remarkable still, this Lola Montez, whom most people (Rudi Schneider included) thought to have been a Spaniard, spoke English with a marked Irish brogue while Rudi (at least in his state of consciousness) was not able to speak anything but German with a very strong Austrian accent. Many witnesses scoffed at the Irish accent and said that the royal mistress was something projected by Rudi's subconscious but all this did not explain the Austrian mechanic's perfect mastery of Anglo-Irish, and the scoffers were more than confounded when it was pointed out that Lola Montez had actually begun her career as Marie Dolores Eliza Rosanna Gilbert, born in Limerick, Ireland.

Rudi Schneider's visit to London was given a great deal of publicity. Leaders of every branch of science and education were invited to come and witness his performances at a scientifically supervised seance in Dr. Price's laboratory.

It was said that if Rudi glared at a table, it would begin to move toward him; if he warned it off, it would back away. He was supposed to be able to hold inert objects suspended in mid-air for as long as he desired and to increase his stature at will by five or six inches.

Interest in the seance was increased when Dr. Price offered to pay one thousand pounds to any magician who could produce the same phenomena as Rudi under similar test conditions, provided he would be prepared to lose the same amount if his tricks were discovered. There was no response, but instead a certain Major Hervey de Montmorency wrote in, saying that he had heard of Rudi's trance personality and that he would like to propose a rather unique test. His uncle, he explained, had told him that in 1840, when he was a young man in Paris, the notorious dancer Lola Montez was his mistress and he, the major, suggested that Rudi be interrogated as to the circumstances under which his uncle had claimed that Lola had tried to murder him.

Dr. Price accepted the proposal. It was arranged that a reply from the spirit of Lola Montez would be taken down in writing so that it could subsequently be compared with the account of the escapade which the major was to prepare, likewise in writing but independently and before the time of the seance.

This gala performance was attended by Professor C. E. M. Joad, the noted British philosopher, as well as Lord Rayleigh, son of the winner of the Nobel prize for physics, and other notabilities. A most ingenious device was used to insure that neither the sitters nor the medium could move and produce artificially the phenomena that were expected. The feet of all those present were shod in metal socks while their hands wore metal gloves which were joined by electric wires, so that, if anyone were to move, an electric light would immediately go on. Rudi sat between Dr. Price and Lord Rayleigh, his legs between theirs, and after some effort of concentration, he actually succeeded in putting himself into the peculiar state of mind which endowed him with exceptional powers over matter.

The first thing the sitters noticed was that the atmosphere became perceptibly colder. Professor Joad told the press later that he saw a spirit hand materialize and that a wastepaper basket rose from the floor and moved at considerable speed across the room, resting for a moment on his head and then depositing itself into the hands of the surprised Lord Rayleigh.

After some further psychic vaudeville of the same general sort, Lola Montez began speaking in a strident whisper, singling out Lord Rayleigh for a discussion of his father's theory of sound, a subject on which the late physicist had written a noteworthy essay. It was difficult to get her to concentrate on the Montmorency matter, for she seemed to sense that there was some sort of test to be carried out. Finally she shot back to a pointed question: "How can I be expected to remember all my lovers? I had several of them in 1840. I do vaguely remember a young Hussar officer from Ireland. I called him Bim but that wasn't his name. I believe it was Francis, but I can't recall the surname. We were both rather young and had many a lovers' quarrel. In one of them, the last in fact, I actually fired a shot at him, but it was wide of mark on purpose. He jumped out the window and broke his ankle. I never saw him again."

Major Montmorency's letter read: "My uncle was Mr. Francis Leigh of County Wexford, a lieutenant in the 10th Hussars. In a fit of jealousy Lola Montez seized his pistol and fired. My uncle jumped out the window."

During the dark days of the Battle of Britain, Air Marshal Dowding, Chief of the Fighter Command, was forced to witness death after death of innumerable young men serving under him in Britain's air force. He became obsessed with the hallucinating mystery of death, asking himself: Where do these departed souls go?

One evening, after he had retired from his onerous duties at the Air Ministry, he was sitting in his study at his Wimbledon home when there came, as if from nowhere, a faint but distinct tapping within the walls of the house.

At first Lord Dowding paid no attention, but it finally dawned on him that the rhythmic repetitions might be spelling out certain words. Taking a pencil he began to decode what came forth, and to his amazement the tapping kept on repeating a certain London address. In spite of his fatigue, Lord Dowding ordered his car and driver and proceeded to the location given.

An elderly woman greeted him at the door of the dwelling, someone he had never seen before. He explained his mission and it appeared that he had been directed to the home of a Mrs. Hill, one of London's most prominent mediums. She suggested that she go into trance and see what message might come from the Other Side.

To begin with Mrs. Hill quoted from a book which Lord Dowding was in the midst of preparing. She quoted accurately the opening line: "Now, therefore, as I lay down my sword, I take up my pen and testify."

There was no way Mrs. Hill could have had access to the contents of the book because it was about the air chief marshal's war experiences and was being guarded with the utmost secrecy since it contained material of vital importance for the defense of the realm.

Then one of his dead R.A.F.-men came through with a message, and then another and another. Lord Dowding was overjoyed. He realized very quickly that he was in a strong position to bring a certain measure of happiness to many bereaved parents and friends of men killed under his command or in action under other marshals.

So for several years his Wimbledon home became the headquarters for the greatest spiritualistic movement England has ever known, and since his retirement Lord Dowding has devoted his tireless energy to what he describes as "awakening into their new life the lads who have made the ultimate sacrifice for us."

As proof of the success he has had in this work it is interesting, if not miraculous, that the messages which have come through have convinced many parents that their sons have survived the shock of death and are continuing to live with them as if they had never died.

According to Dowding's book *Lychgate*, the work of the Wimbledon Circle consists of (a) enlightening and consoling the bereaved, (b) transmission of individual messages from identifiable spirits to their kith and kin, (c) the delivery of addresses, in different parts of the country, inspired by their guides, and (d) "rescue" work, that is to say, helping souls of the astral world who do not know they have left their physical body, or who may need help for any other reason.

A tall grave-faced man with a kindly manner, Lord Dowding is a practical man, not in any way likely to be led away by metaphysical theories. In his record lies the assurance that he is a man who is able at once to tell the essential from the nonessential. He insists that he is nonpsychic and has never experienced any supernormal manifestations whatever. No one who examines his fine service to England could question his sincerity.

Unlike most spiritualists, the Dowding Circle uses mainly automatic writing in the receiving of messages. The sitter takes pencil and paper, inhales his breath a few times in order to clear away foreign thoughts, and then awaits the invasion of the spirit.

When the writing begins some sitters become almost unconscious. Mrs. Gascoigne, one of Dowding's most successful and frequently used mediums, has been examined medically during her trances, and it has been found that she is incapable of any thought processes of her own while in that state.

Often the men enter into the minutest details about things they used to do with their loved ones below. Invariably they show in their messages a desire to establish confidence with the living, as if they were afraid that they would not be recognized.

In the midst of the war, when the agonizing word "missing" was used so often in the casualty lists, the men and women of the Dowding Circle were often able to ascertain whether a boy so reported was dead or alive.

Such was a case in which Douglas Hoop figured. His family lived in the North of Scotland and learned that he was missing. But his mother refused to believe that he was dead, although the War Office held out very little hope for him. So on hearing of the work Lord Dowding was doing, Mrs. Hoop wrote in enlisting his assistance and sending a piece of the lad's clothing for psychometric divination.

By the aid of this the medium received the desired contact. She wrote: "I am breaking through to a youth about twenty years old; studious and thoughtful, yet light-hearted and ever ready to see a joke. Great love of the country and nature. Music means a lot to him. Hesitant in manner, due to shyness which he conceals. Fine open countenance; a boy with a fine soul—spirit well developed. Deeply religious, but has no time for sanctimonious people or anything else he feels disingenuous. Lover of beauty."

All this was retailed to Mrs. Hoop who immediately recognized the character of her son in the description, and eventually word came from the War Office that he had been killed in action. Since then Douglas has been a frequent communicator with the Dowding Circle who carefully record every word and forward it to his parents. In a special message to his mother, he said: "At first I felt stunned and unconscious. I was very troubled in parting physically from those I loved. But Mumsie, dear Mumsie, thanks for your prayers and your love, thanks for both. Don't grieve about me. I am all right. Thanks for the flowers by my photograph. I know you will both be brave and will try to help me. I'll come again soon."

Like many another R.A.F.-man, he has come again and

is perhaps nearer now to his family than when he was alive and with them in the flesh.

AN ETHEREAL POETESS ✿✿✿✿✿✿✿✿✿✿✿

Just before the First World War the Ouija Board had a brief spell of revived popularity. As a parlor game or as a device to communicate with the great beyond, skeptics and believers alike whiled away idle hours spelling out so-called "messages" from this rectangular piece of wood on which the letters of the alphabet are arranged in two concentric arcs while the pointer, a heart-shaped instrument set on two legs, moves about indicating the various letters in due succession. By placing their fingers lightly on the board, two or more persons can experiment with its more or less erratic meanderings.

On July 13, 1913, while out on a shopping tour in downtown St. Louis, Missouri, Mrs. John Curran purchased a Ouija Board for two dollars and seventy-five cents. Agog with curiosity, she and a neighbor, a certain Mrs. Grant Hutchins, amused themselves that evening for an hour or so as the instrument spelled out various commonplace messages.

Mr. Curran, a civil servant in the Department of Immigration, scoffed at the two women for their feminine stupidity in thinking that spirits could communicate with us in such

43

a cheap and vulgar way. They were about to put down the board when, without warning, the indicator began rushing about so rapidly that their eyes had difficulty in following it. As if it had suddenly become endowed with a force of its own, it spelled out a message that made the two women look at each other in nonplused amazement. "Many moons ago I lived. Again I come. Patience Worth my name."

Mrs. Curran seized the board nervously into her own hands, but the apex continued its hasty tracing over the polished surface. "Wait. I would speak to thee. If thou shalt live, then so shall I."

Now Mr. Curran began to take a mild interest in the phenomenon. "Who can she be, this Patience Worth?" he asked laughingly. Then, as if by answer, the following poetic lines were spelled out:

> Am I a broken lyre,
> Who, at the Master's touch,
> Respondeth with a twinkle and a whir?
> Or am I string in full
> And at his touch
> Give forth the full chord?

There followed a brief biography of the spirit's life on earth. She said that she had been a maiden from Dorsetshire. She was born in 1650, the daughter of a weaver and an only child. "My thumb is thick from twisting flax," she wrote and spoke of delivering fine linen to castle folk. After her mother's death she came to America with her father, settling in the vicinity of Martha's Vineyard, near where she was later killed by Indians and "a tree grows out of my grave." Investigations have verified that a woman by the name of Patience Worth actually lived and wrote poems during the middle part of the Seventeenth Century.

Mrs. Curran, who died in 1934, was a woman with mediumistic eyes and a marked spiritual expression. She possessed only an average education and was not a student of poetry. Her sole interest besides her household and her husband was voice culture. By means of Mrs. Curran's Ouija Board, Patience Worth continued to dictate poetry and prose compositions of remarkable literary qualities, always in a language exhibiting all the peculiarities of the period, about which Mrs. Curran could not possibly have had such detailed information.

Mystical poems of great philosophical depth and poetic beauty flowed from the prolific mind in the ether, as for example:

Who would pray, let him then
Make his prayer the sheath of the sword
And not the word. Let him then
Make his prayer the goblet to contain the wine
Yet not the wine. Let him then
Make his prayer a casket of alabaster
In which to keep the jewel, not the jewel.

Enough poetry was collected in a short while for the publication of a book which was called *The Light Beyond* and sold exceedingly well. One evening, while Mrs. Curran was discussing with her husband the welcome financial implications of the Patience Worth success, she casually took up the board, and in quaint archaic expletives this profitable poetess upbraided them for trying to exploit her gift in so selfish a spirit. She announced that whatever money might be made through the sale of her works should not belong to the Currans but was to be used in compliance with her orders or no more work would be forthcoming. "I am a weaver of cloth and this cloth I measure is not for him that hath. Thou shalt take a wee one," she went on, "and thou shalt deliver the goods of me into its hands."

So it was that Mrs. Curran went in search of a baby to adopt. In an indirect way Patience advised her where to go, and she chanced to come across the new-born child of a woman just widowed by her husband's sudden death in an accident. Oddly enough, it had blue eyes and red hair which Patience said she herself had possessed on earth.

Other books were composed by Patience to meet the expenses of bringing up the baby. *Hope Trueblood* became a bestseller in the 1920s. Francis Hackett, renowned for his literary criticism, pronounced the work to be one of great quality, "sensitive, witty, and keenly metaphysical." He joined the ranks of other enthusiasts, declaring that "whoever or whatever Patience Worth is, she meets the tests that human beings have to meet."

The last book to come from the spirit guide before Mrs. Curran joined her was *A Sorry Tale*, the story of the life and times of Christ. Professor Roland Greene Usher, Dean of History at Washington University, has pronounced the book to be "the greatest story penned of Christ since the Gospels were finished." He pointed out that had Mrs. Cur-

46

ran not been a woman of great integrity she would have claimed the distinction of being the author of it for herself; and for the benefit of skeptical critics he declared that it would be impossible even for a scholar to write continually in seventeenth-century English without committing at least minor anachronisms, a thing which never occurred in Patience's writings.

Mrs. Curran seems to have been the sole agent through whom the spirit of Patience Worth could work, and since the former's death nothing more has been heard of her, although automatic writing continues to flourish in one form and another.

THE STRANGE TRIAL OF HARRY NEW &&

Towards the end of 1918, in the City of Los Angeles, that bastion of the occult sciences, a spiritualistic seance took place which was to go down as a unique case in the annals of psychical research.

In a fashionable residence, a group sat round a circle, the lights dimmed, as the medium went into trance. Her body quivered and started; she began uttering little groans as if in pain.

Then under direct observation, a vaporous mist, not very clear, floated before the audience. The spot spread and thickened until it assumed the proportions of a small face. It gradually became well-formed, surrounded by a kind of white veil.

As comprehension dawned on the sitters that it was the materialization of a deceased person, some of them recognized it to be a face they had seen on the front page of the newspapers some time before. It was the living prototype of a murdered girl.

From the depths of the medium's heavy sleep rose the voice of another being—that of a young woman. It moaned out in an agonized pitch: "I am a spirit unknown to you. I must talk about a matter of life and death. My name is Freda Lesser. Please, please, save my fiancé Harry New who is going to be condemned in a few minutes for my murder. But I swear he did not kill me. I loved him too much, and quite rightly he grew tired of me. When I went to see him on that fatal night, I attempted to force a double suicide. His gun went off when he struggled to take it away from me. I beg of you all to do something. Tell him I love him tremendously. I always shall."

Resorption of the ectoplasm followed immediately; the medium started rolling her head with a twitter of returning life. One of the sitters, a prominent lawyer, was the first to speak: "We now have proof that life goes on beyond the grave. This calls for action and it is our duty to report what we have seen and heard to the appropriate quarter."

At that moment Harry New's trial had come to an end and the jury was filing out to consider their verdict. The facts of the case were these:

The accused was a rich young man, the product of the

new Californian gentry made wealthy by the fruitful vines of the sun-kissed state. Freda Lesser and he had become engaged to be married some time before and had been widely feted among the social colony. They had looked forward to a happily married life together, each exhibiting symptoms of one hopelessly in love.

But one day, when they appeared together, Harry was resolutely silent. He was known to be subject to moods, but on this occasion he acted as if he had received some sort of psychological shock. They left the party early; next day it was announced that their engagement was broken off.

Both were reticent about the matter. What little their friends could ascertain was merely that Harry had undergone a change of heart, that he had told Freda that he no longer loved her. It was naturally hoped by all that the two would patch up their differences.

In a little while, however, the break widened to the point of bitterness. Harry's love had turned to hate, but Freda was fierce and unyielding. If she could not have him for herself she was determined that no one else should have him in her stead.

She went to see him. There were violent words between them. A struggle ensued in which the sharp sound of a shot rang out. The police were called by neighbors, and Freda was lying dead with a bullet through her heart. She had been shot by Harry New's gun at close quarters.

Naturally he was charged with the crime of murder. The case seemed a forlorn hope to his counsel. Only a miracle could save him from the gallows. The wisest course was obviously to try to make a "deal" with the District Attorney, but even an offer to plead guilty to get a sentence of life imprisonment was turned down.

Although Harry's story seemed plausible enough, no one would believe it, especially since it came from a young man of the playboy class. He insisted that Freda had come to see him of her own free will and had picked up the gun in a moment of anguish. Realizing that she was trying to implicate him in a double suicide, he wrestled to get the gun away from her and in so doing she was accidentally killed.

The gun showed his fingerprints, a point which the prosecution made good use of. "Here is an open-and-shut case of murder," roared the District Attorney. "You have here a young man, rotten to the core with too much money, who murdered this beautiful innocent girl in a moment of passion, thinking he could buy his way out." Then followed the stereotyped plea for hanging. Never were the dice more heavily loaded against a defendant.

The jury were still out when the lawyer from the seance reached the court. Dramatically he informed the judge that he wished to submit unbiased evidence which might but should not be considered improper to place before the jury. The judge hemmed and hawed, finally overruling the objections of the prosecution.

With no little astonishment the jury listened to the amazing evidence. The judge issued new instructions: "Do we know what it is that dies in the dead?" he asked solemnly, "or even that anything dies? Beyond all doubt there exist phenomena of which we know absolutely nothing. It is by no means impossible for this dead girl to communicate with us in this way. Always hungry for justice, we must weigh this curious evidence. But you must all be guided solely by your own beliefs and must bear in mind that there is no proof on which to base the truth of this phenomenon."

After retiring for an hour the jury returned and announced a verdict of "not guilty."

As for Harry New, he joined the spiritualist cult, knowing that Freda's love would never again be repeated in human form. Through the seances he was able to live with his sweetheart as if she had never died by his gun!

HUMAN BLOODHOUNDS ♻♻♻♻♻♻♻♻♻♻♻

Paradoxically, clairvoyance is illegal in England, but the men of Scotland Yard do not scorn its aid in some of the most difficult cases which come within their province. So it is a fact that they have made use of the services of Miss Nell St. John Montague, the famous society clairvoyant, who claims, by the way, to have been consulted by several members of the Royal Family. It is she who was directly responsible for solving the Irene Munroe case, as brutal a murder as can be found in the annals of crime.

On August 20, 1920, a young boy was playing on a shingled beach between Pevensey and Eastbourne, when suddenly he stumbled over an object protruding from the pebbles. He took one look and ran screaming to his parents.

The father went to the spot and found that the object which the boy's foot had accidentally struck was another foot, likewise human. Uncovering the rest of the body he found that the features by which one usually tells whether a face is a man's or woman's were so mutilated that he shrunk back in horror. Police rushed to the scene and Inspector Mercer, at that time ace investigator of the Yard, was assigned to the case.

Mercer established the identity of the victim as Irene Munroe, a young typist from London, who had been spending her fortnight's holiday at Eastbourne. She came of a respectable Scottish family and was esteemed by all who knew her. There were no clues to elucidate why she had been so brutally done to death. Her purse, with a small amount of money, was left intact.

There happened to be an enterprising young journalist active in crime reporting at the time, who got himself assigned to the case and decided this was an excellent opportunity to carry out a project which he had had in mind for a long time. He wired to Miss Montague whom he knew, asking her to come to Pevensey and use her psychic powers in helping to solve the crime.

In a trance Miss Montague sobbed out a message in the voice of a much younger woman than herself: "I see my murderers in a small hotel. It has a white front and there is an old sign over the entrance. Ask Mother to forgive me."

The journalist handed the results of Miss Montague's seance to Inspector Mercer who scoffed at first. But later he agreed to investigate along the lines of the message. The coastal towns are dotted with small inns but by a process of elimination it was found that only a few had white fronts, and these were finally winnowed down to one named the Albemarle at Eastbourne. There the investigators found two young men, Jack Field and Thomas Gray, who had, it was said, been spending a considerable amount of money. Under intense questioning they finally broke down and confessed to the crime.

Reconstructing the case, the inspector and his collaborators found that Irene had met the two men on the boardwalk in a "pick-up" acquaintance. Her appeal for forgiveness referred to her mother's strict orders never to consort with strange men. Field and Gray had asked her to take a walk along a lonely stretch of beach and as soon as they had come to an isolated spot, one of them had reached for her handbag. She struggled and Gray struck her with his walking cane harder than he intended, knocking her unconscious. Then the two stole most of her money and Field took a huge boulder, dashing it against her face. Both men were hanged in short order.

Another famous crime clairvoyant, the Abbé Mermet has been used to advantage by the police in several countries on the European continent. This man comes from a family with a mediumistic history. His grandmother was well known for her powers of second sight, and his mother too had been gifted in this way.

Mermet was instrumental in putting the police on the track of some of the most dangerous criminals in Europe, including the infamous "Terror of Düsseldorf," Peter Keurten, the German "Jack the Ripper." For a long time the police had been hopelessly dumbfounded by the terrific cunning of this mass-murderer until finally, in great secrecy, the Chief of Police decided to call in the Abbé Mermet.

The first thing the master seer felt from holding a piece of bloodstained clothing belonging to the fiend's latest victim, was that the perpetrator of these vile crimes against women possessed an evil knowledge of a clearly occult nature. It was, Mermet said, most probable that he was gifted with a form of second sight, too. To get "en rapport" with him, however, the seer insisted that he needed some personal article belonging to the hunted man.

This eventually came to hand in the form of a small razor-like knife found near the remains of one of the recently murdered victims. Mermet took it in his hands, holding it close to his nostrils. His breathing became labored, and in a screeching voice he gave exact directions to the hide-out of the killer. Swift action resulted in the arrest and speedy trial of the "Terror of Düsseldorf."

The late Sir Arthur Conan Doyle was an earnest advocate of the use of spiritualism in certain types of crimes. He himself possessed to a marked degree the power of psychometric divination. During the mysterious disappearance of Agatha Christie, the celebrated writer of detective fiction, he reconstructed the whereabouts of the authoress by holding one of her gauntlet gloves, predicting to her husband the precise day and hour on which she would return. It transpired that she was suffering from loss of memory.

Sheriff "Red" Wright of Fort Worth, Texas, has likewise used occult methods of detection with gratifying results. His "human bloodhound" was a Professor Sharpe who will be remembered as the man who told Albert Einstein details of his work about which nobody could possibly have known by normal means. The great scientist dubbed him "the man with fourth-dimensional thought."

The case which Professor Sharpe solved for the Sheriff of Fort Worth was the one in which Emily Farmer, a beautiful society girl, had been murdered. Her body was found lying in a ditch in a very mutilated condition. She had been missing from her home for some time, and her remains were accordingly quite decayed, but not enough to conceal that she had been violently assaulted.

Professor Sharpe took some of her clothing, fingering it lightly, saying quite calmly as he did so: "The man you want for the murder of Emily Farmer is in Kansas City and will be at 254 Cowley Street at 2 P.M. next Thursday." There followed a minute description of the man who, Professor Sharpe warned, was armed.

Immediately the sheriff gave orders to his men to go to Kansas City and enlist the aid of the local police. When Thursday came the little doss house which corresponded to the address on Cowley Street was alive with plainclothesmen.

At the precise hour stipulated by Professor Sharpe, a suspicious and tough-looking man sauntered into the hotel. Spying the detectives he looked furtive and started for the door. As one of them went towards him, he drew his gun and fired, missing his mark narrowly.

He was arrested at once, tried and convicted. Shortly before his execution he confessed to the crime of murdering

Emily Farmer, adding that he did not understand how he could have walked right into the trap set for him at the hotel. He said he had had no reason to go there but something inexplicable had seemed to lure him.

THREE

THE GIRL ON THE TRAIN 💋💋💋💋💋💋💋💋💋

Girard Hale is an American artist whose head of Christ is internationally known. Early in his career he worked for an extended period in Paris. In 1928, he received a commission to do a portrait of Madame Jouvenet (thus referred to by him since he does not feel free to reveal her identity). He had never met her or her husband before, and it was agreed that he should execute the painting in their château on the Loire.

He took the train for the station nearest his destination and found himself at first alone in the compartment. His solitude did not last long, however. He had dozed off for a while, and when he awoke he noticed that a young lady had entered at one of the intervening stations and was now occupying the corner opposite from him. She was rather handsome than beautiful, but in their strangely unstable harmony her features were infinitely more attractive than if they had been modeled upon the strictest rules of symmetry.

There was a remarkable blending of sweetness and mourning in her countenance which did not fail to attract the attention of so observing and sensitive an artist as Girard Hale.

For some time neither spoke, but in a little while Mr. Hale managed to start a conversation by referring to some trivial thing about the journey, and to his great surprise the young woman turned their discussion from general topics to the subject of contemporary painting. The artist was delighted with her amazingly intimate knowledge of his work, especially as he was quite certain that he had never met her before. Her entire manner, while it was far from forward, was that of one who had known him personally for many years.

His surprise was by no means lessened when she asked suddenly whether he could paint from memory the likeness of a person whom he had seen only once or twice. When he did not answer immediately, she continued: "Do you think, for instance, that you could paint me from memory?"

"I think I could, but I would rather do you from life," Hale answered.

The conversation digressed and at about ten miles from Hale's destination the girl got off and bade him a friendly good-bye. "We shall meet again before you have time to forget me," were her parting words.

Arriving at the château, Hale was given a most cordial welcome by his hosts. He was struck by the observation that the Jouvenets were both much older than he had been led to believe. They were really a very elderly couple.

Having dressed for dinner, Mr. Hale made his way downstairs, and in the long corridor leading from his room he almost collided with a young lady who turned out to be none other than his companion on the train. Betraying no surprise at seeing him she greeted him with one of those agreeable joyous expressions that make the plainest woman appear beautiful. "I told you we would meet again," she smiled.

Mr. Hale inquired how she had succeeded in arriving so quickly and added laughingly that he wished he could have come the same way. "That would have been rather difficult," was the cryptic reply. And then, with a gesture indicating that she was in a hurry, she went her way.

At dinner, Mr. Hale spoke of the young woman and how surprised he was to find her there after she got off the train some distance from the nearest station. Monsieur Jouvenet's face darkened. "I can't imagine to whom you refer," he said. "We have no young woman in this house, nor are we expecting anyone."

Hale began describing her appearance in great detail, but when he noticed the strange effect of his words upon the French couple, he changed the subject. His host, however, came back to the topic once more. "Please do me a favor, Mr. Hale," he said after they were seated round the coffee table. "Sketch roughly for me the face of the girl you met."

Taking a piece of paper and a pencil, the artist went to work and soon a hasty sketch developed into the attractive face of a young woman in the prime of life. Mr. Hale was amazed at the ease with which he managed to bring out a perfect likeness of the girl he had talked to on the train and in the corridor. Before he had finished Madame Jouvenet fainted.

"You see," her husband said gravely after his wife had recovered consciousness, "we had a daughter who died many years ago. It must have been she whom you met on the train and in this house, for your sketch from memory bears the most perfect likeness of her."

THE UNFORGOTTEN PROMISE 👧👧👧👧👧👧

The moving picture *Passion* was acclaimed by critics the world over as revolutionary in technique, acting, and directorship, and its star, Pola Negri, became a sensation at once, being proclaimed the greatest actress of the silver sheet.

One of her admirers at that time happened to be a young Pole to whom she felt much attached. A little later his work took him to a distant country where he expected to remain for some years, and a painful parting took place. To mitigate this anguish of separation, the two agreed that if either should die before their reunion, the dead would try to appear to the living.

The man departed. He wrote long letters to his beloved, following the magic-lantern changes in her life with the keenest interest. Miss Negri, however, went to America where she became the leading star in Hollywood films, and the memory of this love affair was quickly forgotten.

One day, many years later, the famous actress was seated alone in the drawing room of her spacious Beverly-Hills home. It was about midday, and the room was full of light. Suddenly some strange impulse caused her to look round. The door was slightly open, and near a large antique couch stood a figure which she recognized at a glance as that of her former admirer.

With a smile of delight she started up and ran forward to greet him, exclaiming: "How could you surprise me so? You never let me know you were in America."

But he waved his hand sadly in a way that forbade approach. She remained rooted to the spot as he advanced a step towards her and said in a low, soft voice: "Do you remember our compact? I have come to fulfill it." And approaching he laid his right hand on her shoulder. Then he smiled a faint, sad smile, turned and left the room, waving a farewell as he passed through the door.

Miss Negri investigated the whereabouts of her friend. As she suspected, he had died very close to the time that she saw his apparition.

THE PERSISTENT SUITOR

Even the cynical Voltaire sang sweetly in his poems of the incomparable talents which Hyppolyte Clairon demonstrated in her acting, and she was considered in her time as great as Bernhardt was in hers.

Like every other famous actress, she was beset by admirers. One of the most ardent was a man in his early thirties, the son of a merchant from Brittany. Mlle Clairon tells the whole story of his strange death and his influence on her life thereafter, in her book of memoirs published in 1800. The facts can also be verified in the Archives of the Prefecture of Police under the reign of Louis XIV.

It seems that young Monsieur de Surat paid passionate court to Mlle Clairon for several years. At first, she received him rather favorably but later became quite cold to his romantic protestations. From what one can gather she must have treated him badly, for in despair he fell into a wasting illness. In his last moments he asked for the happiness of seeing her to say farewell, but she refused and he died alone, except for an old retainer.

On the evening of his death, Mlle Clairon's mother and several friends were supping with her at her apartments in the Rue de Bussy near the monastery of Saint Germain in Paris. Mlle Clairon had just finished singing to her friends when, on the exact stroke of eleven o'clock, a piercing cry of an extraordinary heart-rending quality was heard. Everyone was struck dumb with astonishment and fear.

So violently did it affect the actress that she begged her guests to remain overnight. The next night, at the same hour, further unusual noises were heard, in particular the clapping of hands, followed by sarcastic laughter.

Frightened by this hubbub, she went to the police and asked them to set watchmen, so that the author of the disturbance might be detected. The watchmen were posted, but it was of no avail. Every night at eleven o'clock, the same horrible cry was repeated, sounding as if it came out of vacant air. Everybody, including the police, heard it, but somehow Mlle Clairon knew that it was meant for her alone.

One evening she returned home after dining with a friend. At the very moment he said good night to her on the doorstep, the cry exploded between them. Her friend was quite familiar with the story, which was now going the rounds of Paris, yet it distressed him so much that he fainted and was carried to his carriage more dead than alive.

When the actress got upstairs a horrible sight confronted her. Among the dark shadows she could see Monsieur de Surat. His right arm was raised, as if in menace, but it was his face that held her horrified gaze! It was that of a corpse in the last stage of decomposition. The blue, livid flesh seemed to be dropping off his bones, the thin lips, drawn into a diabolical grin, showed his white teeth in a ghastly line; only the eyes looked alive and imparted to the countenance an expression of despairing hatred, dreadful to see.

Before Mlle Clairon had time to call for help, the awful apparition changed into a shapeless black mass and moved slowly out of her room into the corridor, leaving behind it a horrible charnel-house smell.

The Prefect of Police then took charge of the case. That night he went in person with Mlle Clairon at the appointed hour of the manifestation. Earlier in the day he had pulled up the carpets, sounded the panels of the walls and looked everywhere to make sure no person was hiding there. He arrived a little before eleven, installed himself quietly and waited. Sure enough, at eleven o'clock came an agonizing and awful cry, the cry of a man in the most extreme pain. It seemed to quiver for a moment in the air above them, then went wailing and sobbing downwards; it was followed by the thump of some heavy, solid body dropping close to them. Of course, there was nothing there.

After this the disturbances ceased for a time, and Mlle Clairon joined the theater at Versailles on the occasion of the marriage of the Dauphin. For some reason there were insufficient apartments provided for the cast, and she was forced to double up with an actress colleague, Mlle Grandval. As they were both about to retire she said to her friend: "Here we are almost at the end of the world. Surely it would puzzle the ghost to find us here!"

But before she had finished speaking, the harrowing scream penetrated the whole building. Gowned only in her nightdress, Mlle Grandval rushed downstairs and screamed for the police. But they were as powerless as before.

One day Mlle Clairon was called upon by an elderly lady, who said she was the old retainer who was with Monsieur de Surat when he died.

"All his last days and hours were spent talking of you," she said, "sometimes setting you down as an angel, sometimes as a devil. I constantly urged him to forget you, but he kept on swearing that he would continue to love and hate you beyond the tomb. The passion that ruled him was out of his control, and your refusal to see him in his last moments on earth embittered him exceedingly. He counted those last moments until a few minutes before eleven o'clock, and in a vehement death struggle which terrified me, he exclaimed: 'That vixen. She shall pay for this! I shall pursue her after my death for as long as she held me enthralled in my life time.' I tried to calm him, but with that declaration life had left his body."

After two years and a half, the exact period of his infatuation, the disturbances ceased and Mlle Clairon was left to pursue her career in peace.

WIND UNDER THE EAVES ♂♂♂♂♂♂♂♂♂♂

Standing on a gentle rise surrounded by sweeping lawns, "Pickfair," the home of America's sometime sweetheart, Mary Pickford, and her deceased husband, Douglas Fairbanks, is an impressive sight which is covered in all conducted tours of the homes of the stars of moviedom. Unlike most luminaries of Hollywood, the Fairbanks did not build their home themselves but purchased what was once a shooting lodge. There, before their ownership, some sort of fatality is said to have taken place.

Soon after taking possession Miss Pickford spoke to her husband about some unaccountable noises which she had heard at night. He attributed them to "wind under the eaves," but the roof was replaced along with other alterations, and still the disquieting noises persisted. Considerable pains were taken at different times by both Douglas and Mary, to find an adequate explanation for the sounds; but entirely without success. They were like the pacing of a woman's feet—up and down, up and down.

One night, when the film stars were sleeping in the front bedroom, Mary became conscious of a creepy feeling stealing over her, and the noise in the attic began. Douglas too was aware of a peculiar feeling of suffocating oppression, and both had the strange unearthly sensation that they were not alone.

There was a rustling of the curtains, and then there stood before them near the window, at the far end of the room, a ghostly female, dressed in what seemed to be comparatively modern clothes. She was apparently in great trouble; her hands were clasped and her eyes turned upwards with an agonized look of entreaty.

Douglas was the first to speak: "Mary, do you see that figure there near the curtain?"

"Yes, Doug," she shuddered, seized with fright. When she was asked later on to describe the face, its expression, the color of the eyes, she did so in details that squared completely with her husband's observations.

The same specter has been seen by several guests who have stayed at "Pickfair" from time to time. A titled Scotchman who spent a few days there in 1929 had a more frightening experience even than the one admitted by Mary. On the first night he slept soundly until three, just when the day was beginning to break. He had been awake a short time when suddenly the door of his bedroom opened and shut again rather quickly. Almost at the same time he was startled by the rustling of the curtains, and he distinctly heard someone in creaking shoes pacing backwards and forwards in the large room.

Fixing his eyes in the direction from where the sound was

coming, he saw standing in a corner the female apparition, hands clasped and eyes in supplication. Then she came forward, and to the Scotchman's terror, she touched him on the shoulder with her right hand. It felt icy cold. While he strove to cry out she disappeared.

In an interview back in 1933, Miss Pickford said: "I do not know who this ghost is or what she wants but I know she is here at 'Pickfair.' "

THE SPECTRAL LOVERS 🪰🪰🪰🪰🪰🪰🪰🪰🪰🪰🪰

The former Anna Gould, now Duchess de Talleyrand, lives in her ancestral home on the Hudson near Tarrytown. It is a large pile of masonry brought together about 1870 in the grandiose style of that profligate period, possibly in imitation of a castle on the Rhine. But if history has not had time to hallow it, tradition has not overlooked it. Amongst other remarkable stories, it records that the house is haunted by two spectral lovers.

Many different guests of the duchess, singly and unaware of the experience of others, have told her about having seen two loving phantoms of the same description and of having heard the same sounds. At first she did not believe them, but then one day a particularly hard-headed member of the international set, a person with an eye for reality and wont to see things in life as they actually are (she has married several rich men and lives in New York), replied to the question of how she had slept with a visible effort to sound callous: "Well, I wouldn't have missed it, but your ghost lovers were acting up considerably. I didn't get any sleep at all!" Henceforth that room remained locked up. But here is her story:

She was lying in bed, it seems, with the lights turned off, but somehow she could not manage to go to sleep. After a short time she heard a rustling sound on the threshold, then the hem of a garment seemed to touch the end of her bed. Frightened, she turned on the lights to find that the door had opened quietly by itself but there was no sign of any intruder.

Now the lady got up, locked the door and carefully examined the whole room. She looked under the bed, into the fireplace and up the chimney, in fact everywhere until she was quite satisfied that she had been imagining things and that there was no one else inside the room.

Back in bed, she believes, she may have dozed off into a semi-slumber, but not for very long. Of a sudden she was alerted by a sound resembling the soft tread of a lady's footstep, accompanied by the rustling of a silken gown.

Gradually she became aware that there was a shadow shaping out of the very air and before her eyes appeared the outlines of the figure of a young woman with a beautiful face, gowned in an extremely rich but very old-fashioned nightdress. She seemed to be waiting for someone and was whiling away the time by combing her long black hair which fell over her shoulders like a cloak.

Then, as if from the walls, wainscotted in paneled oak,

there grew another shape, this one of a young man, about the same age with a strange and tragic handsomeness. The two shapes moved towards each other, fell into a clinch in which they remained for some minutes exhibiting a state of high erotic emotion.

It was the female shape that freed herself from the embrace, uttering as she did so a cry which no human voice could imitate but which suggested the words, "Weep! Weep!" She then went into a paroxysm, as though she were struggling for breath still crying the same words, "Weep! Weep!" The male shape looked on agonized, his corpselike countenance wearing an air of fatal resignation.

All the while the occupant of the room was too congealed with fear to interfere actively. More dead than alive she got up and limped to the door for escape. But before she reached it the two shapes were swallowed up in a dark mist.

The Duchess de Talleyrand insists that the lovers are not of the Gould family; they are the ghosts of the son of a former owner of the manse and his mistress. The bedroom was used by them as a rendezvous and both of them died tragically at an early age.

GHOSTS THAT PAY OFF ᭤᭤᭤᭤᭤᭤᭤᭤᭤᭤

The newspapers in England for the last week of September, 1947, were enlivened by details of a ghost hunt as engrossing as it was unique. The owner of the seventeenth-century house of "Woodfield" in Weathercock Lane, Aspley Guise, Bedfordshire, appealed to the Assessment Committee of Luton for a reduction of taxes because the value of his property had been reduced considerably due to the fact that the place was known to be haunted.

Councilor Richards of the Committee, who lives at Dunstable, agreed that if the owner's complaint was founded, it was only right to concede a reduction. Accordingly he ordered an investigation.

In no time at all ghost-layers, independent psychic researchers, pressmen and others flocked to the little village of Aspley Guise. But Mr. Richards was anxious to obtain accurate information and sought the services of a London medium, Mrs. Florence Thompson, well known for her previous investigations of haunted houses.

Mr. Key, the owner of "Woodfield," explained that the house was associated with a terrible tragedy that had occurred there about 250 years ago. The then occupant, who disapproved of his son's choice of a bride, had locked the two lovers in an attic closet and left them there to die. The crime was discovered by Dick Turpin, the famous highwayman, when once he sought refuge at "Woodfield," but he promised silence in return for sanctuary any time he required it.

A former landlord of "Woodfield" informed Mr. Key that one night he had seen the figure of a man wearing a loose gown at the reading desk in the study. On the desk lay a strange book which he, the landlord, had never seen before and the pages of which the visitant turned over at slow intervals. To the left and right of him stood a young man and a young woman. From time to time he looked earnestly into their faces, and as he did so he appeared to heave a deep sigh. The countenances of all three indicated great distress of mind, as if they were trying to come to a decision. At length the man at the desk closed the book, got up, and left the room, with the young couple following close upon his heels. Then there rose in the still night a sound that froze the blood in the tenant's veins. It was a strangled scream, followed by the sound of a door slamming loudly. Then silence again.

Mrs. Thompson, the London medium, had never heard this story, but she was strongly conscious of the ghostly presence of a pair of frustrated lovers. She went into trance and there was a tense atmosphere as the circle of investigators waited for her to speak. Finally the silence was broken by her sobbing and whimpering. Then, expressing herself through the medium, a girl's voice said: "We were going away together, but my father knew about it and laid a trap for us. We were shut up for a long time. I do not know how long it was before our bones were buried."

In her waking state the medium said: "I feel sure that a terrible tragedy took place here long ago. There are indications of two spirits who are in need of help, one of them a girl about twenty."

Convinced, upon hearing this evidence, that there was reason to believe that something superphysical was associated with "Woodfield," the Assessment Committee voted to reduce its taxable value by ten percent. It must be added, however, that these men did not go exclusively by Mrs.

Thompson's testimony. There was, as it were, a good deal of circumstantial evidence, connected with the character of Dick Turpin whose rôle in the "Woodfield" tragedy is at least indirectly corroborated by the fact that he and his horse Black Bess had been seen in recent times—that is, more than two hundred years after his death by hanging in 1739 —by over a hundred witnesses all through the countryside.

One eyewitness tells of having seen one evening an odd-looking individual clothed in the style of a couple of centuries ago, riding along the main highway. Thinking that it must be someone playing a joke or doing it for a wager, he merely watched the rider with curiosity. But suddenly, without paying any attention to the stream of evening traffic, the rider crossed the road in the midst of several speeding motor cars. Certain that both rider and horse would be badly crushed, the observer made his way to the other side, only to see man and horse riding on unperturbed. The car that should have hit them, had passed right through.

One peculiarity reported by another villager who has seen Black Bess and Dick, as the apparition is familiarly known, is that although the horse never seems to slacken its pace, it somehow always manages to keep the same distance away from an observer. This characteristic of Dick's phantom is strangely at odds with the belief far-spread among the hunting set in Bedfordshire that, if a rider has the effrontery to overtake Dick and Bess in the field or on the road, that rider's life is doomed.

THE ABBEY OF SAINT WANDRILLE &&&

The Abbey of Saint Wandrille in Normandy is one of the most majestic and venerable monasteries in France. Standing not far from Caudebec, near a river, it combines, in an enchanting medley, every style of every century from the Twelfth to the Eighteenth. A French gazetteer, which offers a brief description of Saint Wandrille and its historic objects, is the source of this cryptic statement: "There is said to be a secret room in the abbey, known to no more than one monk at a time, who is bound to reveal the secret only on his death-bed, and then only to his successor custodian. Frequently this room has been the object of vain search."

When Maurice Maeterlinck took possession of this landmark, it was under quite strange circumstances, but no wise stranger than the things that were to happen during the great poet's tenancy.

It was at the beginning of the century, and France was in the grip of an administration ferociously anticlerical. All religious properties were made subject to confiscation, but the Church countered by threatening to excommunicate all those who purchased any kind of ecclesiastic property. To avoid this dilemma Monsieur Maeterlinck entered into secret negotiations with the Abbot, and in a rather fictitious sale, he took over the Abbey from the Benedictines and agreed to return it to them within a given length of time.

At Saint Wandrille, Maeterlinck found the realization of

the scenes in which he had set the adventures of his famous princesses, of Melisande, Ygraine, Maleine, and Selysette. Wandering around his new abode to absorb its atmosphere, he saw everywhere remnants of a life that had long ago disappeared. Old doors locked up by leafy shrubs marked the state of disuse into which the old monastery had fallen. A maze of silent passages led from the huge refectory with its barbaric spaciousness to rows and rows of solitary cells.

Outside, the mystic strains of night unfolded like harmonies from a better world; the undulation of the balmy air, the rustling of the leaves, the vague effects of shadow and light on the great building, the chirping of the crickets, the dying twinkle of the rill . . . all these things added to the ghostly impression of the scene.

Monsieur Maeterlinck had heard vague rumors that the abbey was haunted. He felt inclined to take these rumors seriously. A place like this where so many human beings had lived and suffered, he reasoned, must have their history invisibly impressed upon the walls. And it seemed credible enough that some of them should have left behind a palpable reflection of their existence.

On retiring, the poet was unable to sleep. He lay awake, silently soliloquizing, when suddenly he became aware that his room was shared by another. With every instant the certainty grew that there was somewhere near an unwonted and baleful presence.

He got out of bed and reached for his gun, but before he could make light, he saw silhouetted in the gloaming of the arched window a long, chalklike face with flashing eyes. He fired a shot and rushed to the window to look outside.

Hardly a breath of air was stirring; not a leaf trembled, and even the moon shone lifelessly above. Could this have been a deluding dream?

In a few months he had converted the abbey into a quite liveable abode; sacristy closets had become substantial bathrooms, confessional boxes good cupboards, and the antique furnishings were metamorphosed into period pieces.

One of Maeterlinck's first guests was Constantin Stanislavsky, the great Russian actor, who came to discuss with him the matter of producing *The Blue Bird* at the Moscow Art Theater. He was given what was known as the Round-Tower bedroom which once housed an archbishop. During the first night he was kept awake by the vague crumblings and mysterious noises of the sleeping monastery. At five o'clock the noises became so loud that he was convinced that some carpentry work was going on nearby.

Next morning, when Maeterlinck asked him how he had slept, Stanislavsky replied quite cheerfully: "Not too badly. But those carpenters of yours start work very early. They seem to have finished though putting up that scaffolding of theirs, for they are quiet now." Of course there had been no carpentry at that hour, let alone on a Sunday morning.

Another guest was an American woman who was occupying a room in an entirely different wing. The next night this guest awoke the whole household screaming: "I have seen a ghost. I have seen a ghost!" She insisted that she had seen a gaunt, deformed man, dressed in the robe of a monk, who appeared in the center of her room, silent, mysterious and very grim. Crossing himself with his lean yellow hands he had said as he did so: "Madame, prepare for Eternity."

And then he had disappeared as quickly as he had entered.

There happened to be in the party a woman well known for her mediumistic powers, and she suggested that they do a table turn. So after dinner next evening the whole party sat round the coffee table with the lights low and their hands palm downwards.

First the table did not move at all. Then slowly it became animated. It oscillated. Up and down it went. The medium then began questioning the spirits, using the ordinary alphabet for the number of knocks by way of answer.

"Who are you?"

"A monk named Bertrand."

"When did you die?"

"In 1693."

"What do you want with us?"

There came no answer; the table remained motionless. The sitting ended with the party in an unsatisfied mood, but soon wit and humor returned to the circle and the matter was disregarded.

By this time Monsieur Stanislavsky had decided to do some research on his own, and accordingly he looked for evidence. With Maeterlinck's permission he explored the entire abbey. Ransacking the attic of one of the wings he came across a long-forgotten book of records under date of 1745. To his amazement he found in it a reference to a monk named Cornelius who had lived in the abbey at the end of the Seventeenth Century. This monk was called "the Hunchback" because of his crippled spine, and he appeared to have been often in trouble, for the record of his penances was considerable. There was also an entry according to which a monk named Bertrand had actually died at Saint Wandrille in 1693.

Hurrying to the East Gallery, where he remembered having seen some tombstones, Monsieur Stanislavsky found in a cloister a moss-streaked plaque, worn and defaced, on which he could just make out the words: BERTRAND. PAX VOBISCUM. A.D. 1693.

Thrilled with the idea that he might be on the point of making a striking discovery bearing on the question of man's position in the universe, the Russian actor pondered the matter of the disturbances in the night and the apparition seen by the American lady. Could it be that Cornelius was responsible for her fright the night before?

To add to his curiosity, Maeterlinck told him about the legend of the secret room, laughingly suggesting that he find it if he could. In some spare hours he tapped every panel he could find, prying the wainscoting that looked suspicious. It was almost a forlorn hope, for the Abbey of Saint Wandrille is actually larger than a city block. Exhausted, he sat down at the end of the wide corridor of monks' cells, and with a fatal sigh of resignation he tapped one last panel. It echoed hollow.

He gave it a ferocious push and in it went. But instead of a room he discovered only a recess containing something very dusty. In dumb bewildered horror he found that the contents were the mouldering skeleton of a human being with a twisted spinal column. Here were the remains of the refractory monk who evidently had been immured for his sins. At once the experience of the American guest took on a horrible significance.

Further confirmation came some time later when Maeterlinck was advised of the death of the woman as predicted by the ghost of Cornelius.

"THE BROTHER-IN-LAW"   ଔଔଔଔଔଔଔଔ

Professor Montague Rhodes James was Provost of Eton College, the most exclusive boy's school in England. He was the author of some fifty books including *The Ghost Stories of an Antiquary*, and, as though that were not enough to keep his memory alive, soon after his death in 1936, a new building was dedicated to his name.

During his tenure as Provost, Professor James would regale his boys with selections from his repertoir of stories. There was one in particular which, he claimed, had actually happened to him. He called it "The Brother-in-Law," but because it involved a murderer who had never been brought to justice, the Provost felt that it should not be published until after his death. Here is the story as retold a few years ago by an old Etonian who has since made the supreme sacrifice as an officer in a crack regiment of the British Army.

Late one evening Dr. James was alone in his study poring over some ponderous work, when his maid announced a visitor. The name on his card meant nothing to the professor, but the urgency of his business was emphasized by a

scribbled message couched in such words as to make a refusal quite impossible.

A man of about fifty years of age was shown in. He was
tall and distinguished-looking with a lithe, quick-moving
figure. A well-proportioned brow gave a hint of good intellect but seemed furrowed deeply with lines of worry.

"Professor James," he began uneasily, "I have come to
you because I believe you are the only man able to help me.
I have read your books and consider you the greatest living
ghostologist. Still, I do not expect you to believe right away
what I am going to tell you, but before you make up your
mind that I am insane, let me assure you that I am able to
prove every word I am going to say. Before I leave this
room you will have seen with your own eyes that I am
persecuted by a hideous phantom."

During this recital his features had gone a delicate green.
His eyes took on a haunted expression as he continued in a
matter-of-fact tone of voice.

"First I should tell you that I have killed a man. It was a
case of justifiable homicide and I am ready to give myself
up. I do not believe, however, that any court would convict
me of murder.

"About three years ago I married a woman who, as I
learned before long, was suffering from tuberculosis in a
very advanced stage. I did everything in my power to save
her life. I took the best advice available, and for some time
we went to live high up in the Swiss mountains. But finally,
when the doctors told us that there was no hope, my wife
and I decided that she might just as well lead the last lap of
her life as she pleased. We spent some time in Paris, Vienna

79

of the Park. The footsteps behind me echoed in the deepening twilight. Suddenly I purposely stopped in my tracks and pivoted round.

"No sooner had I done so than the figure in the gloaming did the same. In the silhouette I could discern the bulky figure of my brother-in-law.

"I was too dumbfounded to say anything. As I stared at his dark form, it seemed to resemble something monstrous. I nerved myself and took several paces towards him; he moved the same distance away. So I went on, deciding to treat the situation for the trivial thing it was. After all, he was known to be eccentric, and he was obsessed with the mistaken idea that I was responsible for his sister's death. My conscience was quite clear. If he tried to attack me I was quite capable of taking care of myself, being considerably taller and heavier. I did not believe that he would stoop to the device of attacking me from behind.

"So I made haste to the nearest exit, and I can assure you, I was quite relieved when I got to a place from where I could hail a cab and drive to my hotel. But when I arrived and entered the door, I caught a glimpse of my brother-in-law emerging from another cab. I went to the desk to get my key and hurried to the elevator. I fairly collapsed on my bed. I couldn't understand why this silly thing had upset me so.

"That night I could not sleep. My mind continually whirled back into the past; my life with my deceased wife, her words of warning, and the audacity of this man's obsession. The injustice of it all surged torrentially in my mind. Whilst I pondered, I became conscious of a faint but distinct tapping on the wall next door. I thought nothing of it at first, taking it to be some defect in the water system. But it became more and more deliberate, and I was convinced it was being done to cause me annoyance. Finally I called the manager, and on investigation he had a page report to me that the noise was being made by the occupant next door, that he refused to answer the telephone or the door which was locked from the inside, and that I might feel sure that he would desist from sheer boredom before long. In any case he would be spoken to at the first opportunity.

"Next morning the noise had stopped. I felt somewhat better. I left my room at about nine-thirty to go downstairs to breakfast, and I noticed that the door next to mine was ajar which seemed to indicate that a maid was in there cleaning up.

"I sat down at my usual table, and no sooner had I received my coffee than to my great irritation I noticed my brother-in-law sitting with an air of perfect innocence at the other end of the room.

"At last I grasped the studied plan of oppression. He meant to dog my footsteps until my mind would give way. This unnerving thought brought me fully to my senses. I must act fast and meet him with some sort of counterplan.

"I pretended not to notice him, going directly to my room. I was determined to circumvent, if I could, his attempt to unhinge my mind. So I set about moving elsewhere, leaving no trail behind me. It took some subtle legerdemain, I can tell you, but the details do not matter now.

"I duly ensconced myself at a remote hotel in South

and Berlin and finally returned to London, the city of her birth and many pleasant associations.

"The wonderful thing was that she never seemed to get depressed, and I believe that secretly she thought that she would defy the prediction of her doctors.

"Now my wife had an elder brother whom I knew very slightly. He was enormously attached to her, but as we were poles apart and disliked each other, their meetings became fewer, and he developed the obsession that it was I who prevented him from seeing her.

"When we returned to London, he pretended to be horrified. Nothing would convince him of the hopelessness of my wife's condition. Somehow the horrible idea germinated in his diseased mind that I was trying to hasten her end.

"One day I came face to face with him by chance and he challenged me with this unspeakable accusation. Only by maintaining an iron self-control did I manage to avoid a fight. The strained situation between us upset my wife, and I honestly believe that it reduced the number of her remaining days. In her final death struggle, her last words to me were a warning to beware of her brother. 'He has uncanny powers,' she stammered weakly. She was going to say something more but I exhorted her to save her strength, and so I learned no more. In a few minutes she died in my arms.

"It was not long before I was to find out what she had meant. That evening I went to find solace in the evening colors of Hyde Park. I sauntered along with my head bowed in grief, not noticing anything, so stunned was I at my loss. But gradually I became aware that I was being followed. Dusk was descending and I had reached a deserted stretch

Kensington; no one could possibly have trailed me. The papers modestly featured my disappearance in about a week due to the fact that I had left everything I owned at the other hotel. I exalted in my ruse. At last I was going to be alone."

At this point the man's voice became thin and reedy. He had been glancing nervously about the room. He paused a moment to mop some beads of sweat from his forehead. The scared, haunted look in his eyes now dominated the whole face. In less resolute tones he went on:

"But, Dr. James, I was wrong. One night I heard the harrowing and familiar tapping at my wall. This time I did not question it. There was no doubt in my mind as to who was occupying the adjoining room.

"At this stage I was in a state of near delirium. I then and there resolved, in my overwrought condition, to put an end to this vile persecution. I crept out into the corridor. I tried the handle of the room next door. I was amazed when it opened and I entered without hindrance.

"My blood ran cold as my eyes beheld my tormentor sitting in an armchair by the wall holding a blunt-looking instrument which at first glance might have been taken for a broken dagger. His face wore a smug expression as much as to say: 'Well, I've been waiting for you. It's just as I planned it.' His speaking brown eyes, the only thing that commended his countenance, now shone with a fiendish gleam. A close beard concealed the mouth without disguising any of its determination; he did not stir. Maliciously, with a knowing grin, he simulated the movement of tapping with the dagger in his hand.

83

" 'Look here,' I began heatedly, 'this has gone far enough. My conscience is clear about your sister's death. But I am prepared to go to great lengths to stop your vile persecution. I warn you that I shall do something desperate if you do not leave me alone at once.' He did not answer and continued to grin at me with those lynxlike eyes. I addressed him again in more pleading terms; it was no good. Then and there I resolved to take the law into my own hands.

"I sprung at him and in a moment we were scuffling on the floor. He began striking out with the blunt instrument which he still held in his hand. I was amazed at the ease with which I got my hands round his throat; in a moment, which seemed an eternity, his breathing exhausted itself to a mere throb. I didn't let go until it ceased completely.

"I laid out the body on the bed and made my getaway. For hours I walked the streets. I had done a terrible thing but I felt strangely uplifted. After tiring myself out I put up at a hotel which was really only a doss house—a low place in Shepherd's Market. I decided to give myself up the next day, but I wanted just one night's full sleep in order to rest my overtense nerves.

"That night I went to bed at peace with the world, and I said to myself that under the same circumstances I would do the same thing again. For the first time in ever so long, I managed to doze off into restful sleep.

"But I had not slept long before I was awakened by a most peculiar sensation, a feeling as if someone were blowing in my face. Then my ears could hear the distinct sound of breathing. I got up and turned on the light; there was nothing. Back in bed the breathing began again. I reached out in front of me and my hands surveyed the contour of an overnourished human being. It had hands and I felt the clamminess of a face. There it lay beside me, heaving and shivering, invisible to the eyes but horribly real."

In these last minutes the poor man's voice was trembling and tears flooded his eyes. "Dr. James," he cried, "that creature is here with me now. I need not tell you who he is. What am I to do? What am I to do?"

Professor James was in a very confused state of mind himself at this stage. "Let us see things in some form of proportion," he said, trying to help the fellow to pull himself together. "You are suffering from a common hallucination. All you need is the opportunity to unpack your mind. What possible proof have you that this thing of which you speak is here?"

The man seemed to regain control of his emotions for a minute and silently got up, walking to a corner of the room where there was standing a bucket of sand for fire prevention. He spread the sand on the carpet so as to form a little path about five feet long. "All right, I shall give you proof," he said calmly. And taking a few steps along the side of the sand there appeared before Professor James' affrighted eyes the footsteps of another human being which fell with a stumbling, padded tread. "How much longer must I endure this persecution?" the man screamed with a dreadful stare of terror. And right before them the invisible Thing traced in the sand with a spiderlike handwriting the ghastly word F-O-R-E-V-E-R.

FOUR

MUSIC FROM THE DEAD ⚭⚭⚭⚭⚭⚭⚭⚭⚭⚭⚭⚭

Herman Darewski, the composer of many world-famed popular songs, as for instance the incomparable *Whispering*, was touring South Africa some years before his death in 1945, conducting some of his successes at featured concerts. As a diversion one day, he was taken by some friends to see the great sights of nature high up on the Rand. All went well until they encountered one of the torrential thunderstorms common on the Cape.

The party happened to be near a place known as Laing's Nek, noted as a landmark in the war between the British and the Boers, and now an isolated spot. Not far from where their car was being drenched, they espied an old farmhouse which looked not too uninviting as a place for shelter. One of the party knocked at the door, but the house seemed to be deserted, and they finally decided to get in through a window.

Inside they found an amazing scene. No one had occupied the place for many years, and what little furniture there was, had been left in a state of utter disarray. Cobwebs fought with dirt in these surroundings of complete and absolute desolation. In a corner, tucked away as if it were hiding some secret, there stood, of all things, a baby grand piano.

In spite of being wet through, Darewski sat down to play while the storm whined among the crags at the head of the valley outside. Bestowing the touch which distinguished him as an artist, his playing seemed to transcend the thin-bodied tone of the rusty strings. As he harmonized at random his fingers picked out keys blending into an exquisite melody which his friends insisted he must write down for future orchestration.

The party spent the night in the house without incident, and next morning clear weather made it possible for them to continue their trip.

Back in Capetown, Darewski attended an out-of-doors band concert which played many of the customary pieces. He soon became bored and was just about to suggest to his companion that they make their escape, when the band struck up a melody which seemed very familiar, yet he could not place it exactly. Somehow it seemed to belong to his creative mind, but he was certain that he had not composed it. Comprehension dawned on him very shortly that it was the same piece, note for note, that he had unconsciously played on the abandoned piano in the farmhouse.

He rushed up to the band leader as soon as a convenient

moment arrived. "Please tell me who wrote that piece you have just played? You must think me crazy, but I must know!"

"It's rather a strange story," was the reply. "If you come to see me after the concert, I will be glad to tell you."

And the tale unfolded *was* rather strange. It transpired that the band leader had been given the score of the piece by the friend of an old farmer who had composed it and who had died in 1881. This amateur composer had been killed at the first battle of Laing's Nek, and the manuscript had been found among his effects which his friend put away in an old trunk. There it remained for many years until one day the man came across it and felt impelled to send it to the band leader who had broadcast an appeal for musical submissions from the public. It was found to be one of the few pieces with merit and always evoked favorable criticism when played.

THE VACANT VAULT ややややややややや

There is a churchyard on one of the Barbados Islands, which, besides vaults of all varieties, contains a few private chapels, the burial places of some local families of wealth. One of them the visitor will be surprised to find empty. It actually has been that way for over a century, for no one dares to use it for the purpose for which it was built.

Its early history was quite normal. The first incumbent was a Mrs. Goddard who was laid to rest there in 1807, to be followed by a relative of hers, a certain Miss A. M. Chase, who was joined in turn by Miss D. Chase early in 1812.

At the end of that year the vault was opened to receive the body of the Hon. T. Chase. What met the eyes of the undertaker in his preliminary visit was a rather terrible scene. He found the first three coffins opened and the corpses lying about in quite disrespectful positions. This was a rather inexplicable affair because the coffins were all made of lead, as is the common practice in tropical countries.

However, the body of the Hon. T. Chase was interred and the vault sealed up again.

In 1816, a Mr. Brewster, another relative of the same family, died suddenly and the vault had to be opened once again. This time the coffins were strewn about as if a hurricane had hit the place.

Word about this shameful desecration of the dead soon leaked out and public opinion became aroused. Lord Combermere, then governor of the islands, ordered a thorough investigation.

No trace of human footsteps could be found, and the most careful scrutiny detected no secret entrances. Thomas Chase, one of the occupants, had been a man of cruel character who might have had a vengeful enemy in the form of some superstitious servant. But the corpses showed no sign of Voodooism, such as wounding or defiling, and furthermore, this somewhat shaky theory could not explain why the bodies of Mrs. Goddard and the Misses Chase had been treated in the same abominable way.

Lord Combermere came to the conclusion that the vault should be tested for ultramundane influences. He ordered that sand be sprinkled on the floor and the coffins be placed in rows along the walls. The entrance was cemented and a guard placed in front of it.

Some eight months were allowed to elapse, and on April 18, 1820, the vault was reopened in the presence of the governor. The spectacle was again one of frightful desecration. All the coffins were in a most bewildering state of confusion. The seal and cement of the entrance were found to be absolutely undisturbed. There were no traces of footmarks on the sanded floor, and one of the coffins was found jamming the entrance, standing on its head.

Since no human agency could be proved to have anything to do with these weird manifestations, Lord Combermere's only course was to recommend that the Chase family take their dead and bury them elsewhere.

Many years later, Sir Arthur Conan Doyle became interested in the mysterious happenings of the Chase vault. He decided one winter to go to the Barbados partly for a holiday but mainly because investigation of the mystery appealed to him. So in December, 1918, he took ship and made lengthy probes into the mystery, applying to this case the type of deductive reasoning for which his fictional Sherlock Holmes has become famous. But the result was almost nil.

Research of the local records revealed that two of the occupants of the Chase vault had committed suicide, and Sir Arthur veered finally to the interesting theory that when a life is cut short before its appointed time, there remains a store of unused vitality which is capable of working itself off in unusual ways.

His report winds up with the assertion "that the disturbances were the work of forces desiring the more speedy decomposition of the bodies."

REMEMBERING THE FUTURE ✍✍✍✍✍✍✍

On June 18, 1942, under a dead sky and a sullen fog which a strong wind could not dispel, a large American Airways passenger plane, scheduled for Los Angeles, stood ready to take off from the Washington, D. C., airport. Mr. Joseph Szigeti, the internationally-known violinist, entered the huge ship in a tearing hurry. He fell into his seat, heaving a sigh of relief that he had arrived just in time.

Uniformed attendants stood quiet, decorous but vigilant at the entrance. From the gangplank a smartly-dressed woman appeared in a state of excitement. She fairly ran towards the purring plane. There was a slight commotion at the entrance, and in a trice she was aboard. An official of the airline followed her to Mr. Szigeti's seat. "Sorry, Sir, but here is a lady with a priority higher than yours. She has to supersede you."

A sympathetic smile was painted on the refined features of the beautiful blonde's face. By a hardly perceptible piece of legerdemain Mr. Szigeti's bags were seized and he himself hurried out. Seconds are precious in a case like this; there is no time for apologies.

Back in the waiting room he heard the revving of the giant engines. The earth trembled; a wave of dust rose up. A look from the starter's resolute face and then the ship was speeding down the field and soon disappeared into space.

When the starter passed through the door, Mr. Szigeti asked the name of the lovely passenger and was told it was Carole Lombard, the film star. In a few hours the world was shocked by the news of her death in that very plane.

What was the clemency of chance that saved him and sent another to her tryst with a horrible and undeserved death? There is no answer to this sort of question, and rather than try to clear up the matter, we must refer to an earlier event which can only serve to let it appear still more mysterious.

It seems that the deceased film star had a curious configuration of lines in the palm of her hand, which was noted by a celebrated palmist known as Cheiro, whose real name was Count Louis Hamon. After an interview which Miss Lombard had with him in 1934, the seer remarked to his wife: "That poor girl has a terrible end in store for herself! But I see her dying like a heroine. I hadn't the heart to rob her of her zest for life, so I didn't warn her. In any case what use would it be? She has the line of fate on her right palm cut right in two."

This is the same Cheiro who had become famous overnight in America by a very odd occurrence back in 1893. He had arrived some time previously from his native Ireland and had opened a studio on Fifth Avenue in New

York City. He had established a very excellent reputation for the accuracy of his predictions in Europe, but in the United States nobody knew his name. He was just on the point of packing up to return home when the door opened and a pretty, businesslike brunette stepped in. She explained that she was from the New York *World* and that her editor had sent her with a strange proposition. "If you accept, it will make you famous or infamous overnight," she laughed.

Then the reporter went on to explain that she proposed to bring him several palm impressions and that he, without knowing whose they were and without asking any questions, would analyze them and try to prophesy on their basis. All he said would be published, no matter how wrong he might be, and the affair would be given the widest publicity beforehand in order to stimulate interest.

Such a test would have been a big risk for the average palmist, but that was precisely what Cheiro was not.

The palm impressions were brought to him and the test proceeded. After laboring for hours and calling accurately the biographies of such men as the Mayor, the District Attorney and other notabilities, he stopped short when the next and last one was handed to him for analysis.

"There is something in this palm so abnormal and awful that I refuse to read it unless you assure me that my reading will not be published."

It was agreed that the decision would be left to him after he learned whose palm it was.

"This is the hand of a dangerous criminal, a homicidal maniac," Cheiro said gravely. "He has probably committed

93

many murders and is likely to commit many more unless apprehended. If caught it will be revealed that he has used preternatural intelligence to obtain money by murder."

This last handprint was that of Dr. Henry C. F. Meyer, who was at that time awaiting execution in the Tomb's Prison after his conviction for poisoning several of his patients.

Cheiro predicted the abdication of the Duke of Windsor in a book published in 1927. After examining the peculiar astrological combinations which made the prince's character so difficult to understand, he said: "It is well within the range of possibility that the Prince will fall a victim to a devastating love affair. If he does, I predict that he will give up everything, even the chance of being crowned rather than lose the object of his affection."

LINCOLN'S DREAM   ಈಈಈಈಈಈಈಈಈಈಈಈಈಈ

Abraham Lincoln's belief in superstitions is well known, but not enough attention has been paid by his biographers to the significance which the number seven played throughout his career. He considered it his lucky number. His Christian name and surname each have seven letters; he became a member of the House of Representatives on December 17, 1847; he was elected by the people seven times (four times to the Illinois Legislature, once to the House of Representatives and twice to the Presidency); he was shot on April 14 (7 times 2), and his body left Washington on April 21 (7 times 3).

Mrs. Lincoln recalled some very strange incidents of occult origin after her husband's murder. Once in Springfield, for example, just before the election of 1860, she saw a double reflection of Lincoln in a mirror, one quite lifelike and the other ghostly. And this peculiar dual image appeared again just before they left the White House for Ford's Theater on the fatal night of his assassination.

As if clairvoyant, Lincoln brooded over his end. His law partner, Herndon, records that Lincoln said to him several times over a period of twenty years: "I am sure that I shall meet with a terrible end." In Philadelphia in 1861, at Liberty Hall, touching the principle of the Declaration of Independence, he said: "If this country cannot be saved without giving up that principle . . . I would rather be assassinated on this very spot than surrender it." Four years later it was there that his body lay in state.

Perhaps the strangest premonition that the Great Liberator ever had was a dream which he himself recorded on a piece of paper about ten days before he died and which was found on his desk afterwards. The prose bears the mark of his unmistakable lapidary style.

"About one week ago," he writes, "I retired very late. I could not have been in bed very long when I fell into a slumber, for I was very weary. I soon began to dream. There seemed to be a deathlike stillness about me. Then I heard subdued sobs, as if a number of people were weeping. I thought I left my bed and wandered downstairs. There the silence was broken by the same pitiful sobbing, but the mourners were invisible. I was puzzled and alarmed. What could be the meaning of all this? Determined to find the cause of a state of things so mysterious and shocking, I kept on until I arrived at the East Room and entered.

"There I met with a sickening surprise. Before me was a catafalque on which rested a corpse wrapped in funeral vestments. Around it were stationed soldiers who were acting as guards; and there was a throng of people, some gazing mournfully at the corpse, whose face was covered; others were weeping pitifully. 'Who is dead in the White House?' I demanded of the soldiers. 'The President,' was the answer. 'He was killed by an assassin's bullet.' Then came a loud burst of grief from the crowd which awoke me from my dream. I slept no more that night; and although it was only a dream, I have been strangely disturbed by it ever since."

THE DEATH OF SIR HENRY WILSON &&&

Lord and Lady Londonderry divide their time between their palatial Irish estate Mount Stewart and Londonderry House, Park Lane, London. In April 1922, they were entertaining at Mount Stewart Field Marshal Sir Henry Wilson, a gifted Irishman whose name will long be remembered by the British Army.

He had the Irishman's birthright of eloquence and charm added to great military prowess. In 1914 his part in organizing the first BEF to France was so important that the French often referred to it as the *corps d'armée Wilson*, and his popularity with French military leaders, especially Marshal Foch, led to his appointment as principal liaison officer between them and the British army heads.

After the war he entered the slippery domain of Irish politics, becoming Member of Parliament for North Down, and his maiden speech in the House of Commons was marked by such brilliant oratory that his political future seemed definitely assured.

Soon afterwards occurred his visit to the Londonderrys. He had crossed the water with his wife for a few days' vacation at Mount Stewart, for he had finally consented to take a much-needed rest, and also wished to make an informal appearance in his constituency.

In the middle of the night before the Wilsons were scheduled to leave again, Lady Londonderry awoke from a terrible nightmare, crying loudly: "Sir Henry has been murdered. Someone must tell Lady Wilson." She recalls that the dream was so vivid, she saw the murder in its minutest details: two short men firing revolvers at their victim point-blank, and the strangest thing of all, Sir Henry was quite alone and seemed to be trying to defend himself with a long sword which for some reason he carried with him.

Lord Londonderry soon calmed her, assuring her that Sir Henry was safe and sound in the house, a fact which was verified in the morning at breakfast when he seemed never healthier or happier. Lady Londonderry told him about her dream and the matter was laughed off.

On June 21, only ten days after the dream, Sir Henry officiated in full-dress uniform at the unveiling of the War Memorial at the entrance of Liverpool Street Station in London. Returning alone to his home in a taxi he alighted and as he walked up the steps of 36 Eaton Place, two Irish gunmen fired at him from a distance of about thirty feet. Their first shots missed and Sir Henry drew the sword at his side and rushed at them. A second volley sent him sprawling, mortally wounded, to the pavement.

Naturally Lady Londonderry was obsessed by her nocturnal premonition, which she records in her autobiography *Retrospect*. An interesting fact deduced from the murderers who were later hanged, was that the plot to kill Sir Henry was made at the precise time of Lady Londonderry's dream.

LORD DUFFERIN'S COFFIN ✠✠✠✠✠✠✠✠✠

Over the little town of Ballinrobe in County Mayo, the Irish sun had been blazing all day in August 1893, but with the approach of midnight came a refreshing breeze. The Marquess of Dufferin was holidaying from his post as Ambassador to Paris and staying at the home of a friend. He could not sleep, so oppressive was the heat, and he got up to stand on the balcony of his bedroom for a few minutes.

A full moon illumined the sweeping greensward down to the brook which rushed swollen and foam-flecked beneath the garden bank, filling the night with strange eerie noises which suggested choked human voices, now rising into angry threatenings, now dying away in sobbing murmurings.

As Lord Dufferin's gaze sped through the shadowed country beyond, it was quickly brought back to the greensward where now he could plainly see a man walking with automatic steps and wheeling in front of him a barrow across which lay something large and oblong. When the figure came within closer scrutiny, the marquess felt a shudder as he realized that the thing on the barrow was a human-size coffin. The man was young and had a long, thin face with a straight nose, such as was characteristic of the native Irish workmen. And as he went wheeling on, he pushed the barrow from the grass onto the gravel drive, making a gritty sound.

Next morning Lord Dufferin naturally asked his host about the strange scene, inquiring if there were any funerals to take place in the district. But although all the ground employees were questioned, no satisfactory explanation could be found. No one would have any reason to transport anything at that hour, let alone a coffin. So Lord Dufferin agreed reluctantly that he must have had an hallucination, and in a few days he was back at his post, and the affair had gone from his busy mind.

Two months later the marquess was attending with his wife a formal reception in Paris at the Continental Hotel.

A steward ushered them to the elevator, at that time a modern innovation, but as they were about to enter, Lord Dufferin clutched his wife's arm in a gesture of refusal. He gave some excuse—the car being too crowded—but what actually deterred him was the extraordinary resemblance of the operator to the man whom he had seen wheeling the coffin up the greensward of his friend's estate at Ballinbore. The sudden shock gave him an ominous feeling.

As the elevator began moving upward, Lord and Lady Dufferin heard the sound of straining cables; then came a reverberating crash simultaneous with the sound of muffled screams . . . When it was possible to extricate the passengers it was found that all were alive though some of them seriously injured. Only the operator had been killed.

Naturally the premonition of Lord Dufferin attracted attention and the newspapers of the day featured the story. Inquiry about the elevator man was not without its curious side. The authorities found that his papers were missing and his references so obscure that his identity was never established.

THE CURSE OF THE BREADALBANES &&

The earls of Breadalbane have figured prominently in Scotch history for many generations. The original earl invaded Caithness in 1677, when he was plain Sir John Campbell. He did so with such thoroughness that King Charles the Second bestowed upon him the higher rank.

Among some drastic reforms which Lord Breadalbane instituted in his new domain, was an order to burn all witches within his boundaries. This edict resulted in the burning of a poor old woman on Loch Tay, who, as she died under the crackling flames, screamed a curse resounding in the Breadalbane family to the present moment. "I suffer now," she mouthed in agony, "but the Breadalbanes will suffer always. Long may their name last, and wide may their lands be, but never shall their heirs inherit as father to son."

The first Earl of Breadalbane may have mocked the poor sufferer. If he did, time, that inexorable avenger, was not slow in proving that he was wrong.

His son went insane and was passed over in succession. By special arrangement with the King, the letters patent were altered to include a clause in favor of the heirs male-general, that is to say that the title could devolve onto any male kinsman, not necessarily from father to son as is stipulated in most letters patent.

Accidents, diseases, and wars carried off in a most relentless way the potential heirs in the Breadalbane family. The third Earl died of a mysterious illness which could not be diagnosed and left no issue. So the honor was received by his cousin, Sir Robert Campbell. This gentleman had a son who died in infancy by a fall from his cot. The fifth earl was found dead in a lonely copse where he had been shooting rabbits. He, too, left no issue so that his cousin, also a Campbell, succeeded him. This new incumbent died again without kin, and it looked as if the witch's curse had finally run its course, for all known branches of the family had died out, and the title was in danger of becoming extinct.

Some years later, however, in 1872, John Alexander Campbell filed a claim in the House of Lords in an effort to take the title out of abeyance. He was able to prove that he was a very distant collateral of the Breadalbanes. On the strength of this he was granted permission to inherit the title and estates in Caithness. He evidently expected to raise a large family and in preparation for it he enlarged the castle by the addition of a new wing. Yet he died childless.

The same fate was in store for the seventh earl, Charles William Campbell, who died in 1923. He made every effort to beat the curse by insuring that his nephew and heir, Ian Edward Herbert Campbell, would marry early and thus sire himself an heir, nature (or the witch's curse) having deprived him personally of any issue.

It was with considerable alacrity that news of the birth of his great-nephew was received, and the old earl died happy in the thought that the witch might at long last be ditched. Subsequent events point to that possibility, for both the new Earl of Breadalbane and his son, known as Lord Glenorchy, have endured risks in their lives which might tempt Providence, let alone a witch's curse.

During the first World War, Lord Breadalbane went to France with the Second Division, commanding the c93 Battery, was badly wounded in the retreat of Mons and was for some time reported dead. Back in the base hospital he rallied, and after a short rehabilitation period he was soon again in the field. In fact he became known as the man whom the Germans couldn't kill, having been under fire at such shambles as Basses Maroilles, Villers Cotterset, Marne, Loos, Beaumont-Hamel, Vimy Ridge, and Messines.

In the second World War, Lord Glenorchy was one of the first to go overseas and received his commission as a lieutenant in the Black Watch regiment. He fared forth with them to India where he distinguished himself in the terrible cyclone and tidal wave which swept over the Mindapore area in Bengal Province.

In the midst of this cataclysm the Highlanders were forced to wade shoulder-deep through flooded village streets in an effort to rescue the stranded natives. The gallant lord cleverly rigged up a little craft in which time and again he crossed the wild crocodile-infested waters, many times coming close to the jaws of death, but he survived and may well be the first and only Breadalbane to inherit the title and estates from father to son.

THE CURSE OF MOY 🐦🐦🐦🐦🐦🐦🐦🐦🐦🐦🐦🐦🐦🐦

One of the last British officers to be killed in the First World War was the only son of the Mackintosh of Moy and Mrs. Mackintosh. The event reminded Scots folk painfully of that Curse of Moy which is the theme of a ballad in Scots minstrelsy.

The Clan Chatham and the Clan Grant were long at war

in a hateful vendetta. In one of the many encounters, a Mackintosh killed the father and brother of the Chatham heiress whom he brought to the bloody scene in order to force her to look upon it. The young girl, no more than a child, was considered fey, and her powers of second sight were known to be remarkable. Turning her eyes towards heaven after beholding her beloved dead, she uttered a curse which the ballad records as follows:

> Never the son of a Chief of Moy
> May live to protect his father's age,
> Or close in peace his dying eye,
> Or gather his gloomy heritage.

And it is a curse that has worked throughout the centuries. With monotonous regularity no Chief of Moy has been succeeded by his own son. One by one they have lived to bury their male heirs. In recent times the Mackintosh of Moy came into the estates from a brother who had married the eldest Miss Graham of Netherby and died a few months later before the birth of his son.

THE BLEEDING SWAN ৬৬৬৬৬৬৬৬৬৬৬৬৬

During her reign the Empress Eugénie was very minor key about a singular fact concerning her genealogy. She came, on her mother's side, from a family of Scots gentry named Kirkpatrick and was inclined to cloak this as much as possible by the great name of her father, the Count of Montijo, grandee of Spain. Her parents had met and married at Malaga, where her mother's father (a naturalized American citizen) had a wine distillery which he operated in addition to his work as American consul.

Little would Eugénie ever have cared to cultivate her Scots relatives, had she and the Emperor not been driven to seek asylum in England after the fall of the Second Empire in 1870, and even then she might not have done so, if a very strange thing had not happened at the time of the Emperor's death at Chislehurst, on January 9, 1873.

The fallen monarch was lying very ill after a serious surgical operation and Eugénie was awaiting the bulletin of his doctors while strolling nervously to and fro in the grounds of her mansion. On the lake her eyes were attracted by the sight of a lone swan, and she remarked about it to her lady-in-waiting, for up to that time no swans had been seen at Chislehurst. As the large bird swam toward them, the Empress started back. "Look," she cried, "the swan has been injured. It is bleeding at the breast." The lady accompanying her noticed the very same thing, but before they could call a gardener to attend to the suffering bird, news came that the Emperor was failing, and the matter of the swan was forgotten.

Some years later, in 1879, while the Empress was playing whist, she again saw the swan from the huge windows facing the lake and someone commented that there was a blood-red mark on the bird's breast. This time the Empress gave orders that the gardeners should see what had happened to it, but by the time they arrived at the scene, there was no sign of life on or around the lake. Within twenty-four hours, the Empress received a telegram that her son, the Prince Imperial, had fallen to the assagais of a Zulu in Africa while out on a reconnaissance patrol with the British army.

Realizing now that the appearance of the swan had some deep significance, the Empress, an intensely superstitious person, became alarmed. She decided to leave Chislehurst, the scene of so many painful memories, and purchased a baronial hall at Farnborough Hill in Hampshire, where there was no lake and, in fact, no water within a large radius. Here she lived from 1881 onwards, building a splendid mausoleum right on the grounds to house her ill-starred dead.

At about this time she became acquainted with her British collateral, possibly in quest of an explanation of the swan phenomenon. One of the Kirkpatricks, an old spinster living at Dumfries, regaled her with the family legendry including an odd but interesting story which seems to offer a complete explanation of the curious death warning.

Closeburn Castle, the ancestral home of the Kirkpatricks, was surrounded, or nearly surrounded, by a large lake which served in olden times as a defense and also as an ornament, and it was, at one period, adorned by two graceful swans. Due to the old belief that swans live to a very great age, the local rumor was that the same swans had been there for over a hundred years, and they were revered by everyone.

At the turn of the Nineteenth Century, Closeburn Castle rejoiced in its future owner, a promising youth, not quite thirteen years old and actually as mischievous a stripling as could be found in the vicinity. During his holidays from school, his parents took him to see *The Merchant of Venice* in which he became intrigued with the reference to a swan singing when it died.

Impelled to verify the idea in boylike curiosity, he took his crossbow on returning home one evening and aimed at one of the white-feathered creatures on the lake. The arrow lodged in the breast of the foremost swan which floated, bleeding crimson on its down, to the shoreline. Horror-struck at the thought of what would happen to him when his evil deed was discovered, the young man hurriedly buried his prey. Its companion fled, never to return.

It was at the end of the season, and so the swans were not missed until the following spring when none appeared. But a year later the gardener reported delightedly one day that he had sighted a lone swan on the lake. A feeling of joy, mingled with remorse, sprang up in the boy whose more mature nature now recriminated against his past behavior. But as he gazed at the stately bird he saw that there was a blood-red stain upon its breast. That night, his father, the Laird of Closeburn, died without any previous symptoms of disease.

Thereafter the swan was never seen except as an augury of death, but on such occasions it was sure to make its appearance, coming from no one knew whence and passing as mysteriously to no one knew whither.

In 1920, the Empress Eugenie was in Madrid where she died while staying with her nephew, the Duke of Alba. One of the letters which she did not live to read was from her close friend, Dame Ethel Smyth, who had been to Farnborough Hill in order to supervise some alteration project for her imperial friend. She wrote: "I must tell you something rather odd. On the lawn, near your little summer house, I saw a great white bird which, if there were any water nearby, I would have said was a swan. It was apparently unable to fly, but before I could ask the gardeners about it, it seemed to go into the hedges."

THE LUCKS OF ENGLISH HOUSES &&&&&

Many of the old country houses of England perished in the blitz, but it is singular that a group of the most stately homes in Cumberland, an area which was many times a target of Nazi attacks, has emerged untouched. Antiquarians point to the "lucks" which mysteriously protect these places.

Well guarded and preserved, these talismans are often stored for greater security in the strong rooms of banks.

Their origin is legendary, but their safekeeping is held to insure the safety and good fortune of the home; loss or breakage can mean disaster to both.

The most famous of these weird objects, the Luck of Eden Hall, belongs to the mansion of that name on the River Eden in Cumberland. Its history says that at some unspecified time the butler of the household, while on his way to draw some water at the Spring of St. Cuthbert, found a group of fairies disporting themselves on the rim of the spring. In the midst of this frolicsome circle he observed a curiously painted cup which he seized in spite of the frightened little people. As they ran away, they delivered this parting warning:

> If that glass either break or fall
> Farewell the luck of Eden Hall.

Since the time of Henry the Sixth, Eden Hall has been in the hands of the Musgrave family who have zealously guarded the magic cup. It is a beautiful example of enameled glassware of a yellowish-green hue.

A buzz bomb fell within a hundred yards of the Hall in the late war but the cup, the "luck of Eden Hall," protected it as it had done during other devastating attacks in the district.

Some years ago the "luck" itself had a narrow escape from destruction when the Duke of Wharton, a guest of Sir Christopher Musgrave, accidentally let it fall. An alert butler, however, caught it.

The Luck of Workingdon Hall in Cumberland, traditionally said to have been presented to the Curwen family (and still in their possession) by Mary Queen of Scots, is an agate cup in a perfect state of preservation.

Legend has it that the Luck of Muncaster, which for centuries has preserved Muncaster Castle, also in Cumberland, was given to the owner by Henry the Sixth when he "was in flight and sore distress and found asylum there." It is a fragile glass bowl and is now the property of Sir John Ransden, who feels particularly grateful to it for having saved Muncaster when some neighboring houses were demolished by German bombers.

The Luck of Woodsome Hall, family seat of the Earls of Dartmouth, is a herald's trumpet made of an amalgam of tin and brass, delicately ornamented and bearing the inscription "Simon Belae, Londini. Fecit 1661."

Any time the house has been leased, there has been a clause in which it is stipulated that the "luck" should not be moved, and when in March, 1922, the Earl of Dartmouth sold the house to Mr. Percival Griffith of Sandridgebury, the latter refused to consummate the deal unless the earl would include the priceless trumpet. Failure to blow it on certain occasions is said to presage misfortune.

By far the oddest "luck" of all is the so-called "Screaming Skull" of Bettiscombe House, near Bridport, Dorsetshire. The story of this eerie object is that it was actually a human skull and belonged to a negro servant of the family who was originally buried in a little cemetery right on the house grounds. As long as he was interred there, however, fearful screams proceeded from the grave; the doors and windows of Bettiscombe House rattled and creaked; strange disturbances were heard all over the place, and there was no rest for the family until one of them got the idea to dig up the coffin. For many years it was kept in the cellar and in process of time the superstition that the skull was the luck of Bettiscombe House gained ground and became famous. The rest of the skeleton, all save this relic of the old negro, somehow disappeared, and in his book, *Skull Superstitions*, William Andrews states "that if it be brought out of the house, the house itself will rock to its foundations."

FIVE

WHEN THE BANSHEE STRIKES ৬৬৬৬৬৬৬

There is hardly a family in Ireland unable to contribute some story relative to that aristocratic species of fairies known as the banshees. They are thoroughly and essentially Irish, "ban" meaning woman and "shee" fairy. A banshee is attached to any self-respecting Irish family. She has been described as young and beautiful; or again as an old and fearsome hag. Mostly she is said to be thin and tall with long hair, and generally she is attired in white. She has been seen doing such chores as washing human skulls or bloodstained clothes and reveals her presence by singing in a mournful tone of voice or uttering piercing cries.

Lady Gregory, the famous playwright and the authoress of a book on banshees, is one of the few persons to have been warned by her own. Back in 1932, she was entertaining some friends at Coole Castle, her country home near Dublin, and among her guests was the late poet, W. B. Yeats, himself a keen student of Irish folklore. The house party was assembled for dinner with the exception of the poet who was notorious for being late. Suddenly he came running downstairs and, placing his hand before his eyes as though overcome with terror, he was unable to speak for several minutes. When he had finally regained control of himself, he said: "I have just seen a frightful apparition with the face of nothing that could ever live, or nothing that could ever die. A mass of red hair fell to her shoulders and her eyes—I shall never forget her eyes. They might have been really beautiful if they had not been so hellish in their gaze."

Lady Gregory went white. "That is a perfect description of my family banshee," she said gravely. "It means that someone very close to me is going to die very soon."

Within a week Lady Gregory herself was seized by death.

Yeats never forgot the incident. Seven years later at Cape Martin in Southern France, where he was spending the winter, the poet was recovering from a slight indisposition and determined one afternoon to walk to a little church not far away from the hotel where he and his wife were living, planning to return in time for tea. He was in the habit of going there to sit in the pretty cemetery for a little meditation.

Just as he arrived a soft rain began to patter on the trees, and so he walked straight up the path, bordered with moss-flecked graves and tombs, to take refuge inside the church. Reaching the door he was moved by some indefinable impulse to turn round. With no little amazement he saw seated on a low tabular tombstone close by, a lady with her back to him whom he had not noticed before. She was wearing a black velvet jacket with a narrow border of vivid white; her head of luxuriant jet-black hair was surmounted by a hat also of black velvet.

Actuated by a desire to attract her attention and induce her to look towards him, he noisily opened the rusty latch, and turning round again to see the result, he found that the lady had vanished.

Undaunted he went to the place where she had been and closely searched the area; there was no trace of the late presence of a human being.

The following day, on January 4, he wrote to his friend Lady Elizabeth Pelham: "I know for certain that my time will not be long." He was quick to recognize the banshee warning and he closed his eyes forever on January 28, 1939.

UNLUCKY THIRTEEN ✧✧✧✧✧✧✧✧✧✧✧✧✧

In August, 1885, Sir John Millais, the English artist of immortal renown, gave a dinner in honor of Matthew Arnold. It happened that one of the guests could not be present, and the company present was forced to sit down at a table set for thirteen. Sir John expressed some fear of the possible sequel, but Arnold laughed it off, saying: "The idea, I take it, is that whoever leaves this table first will die within a year. So, with the permission of the ladies, we will cheat the fates for once. I and these strong fellows (pointing to his friend Edgar Dawson and another) will rise together and, I think, the three of us will be able to stand the assaults of the reaper."

Six months later Matthew Arnold died suddenly at the age of 66. A few days afterwards the unnamed friend was found dead in bed. The next to fall a victim to the superstition was Edgar Dawson who was drowned when the ship in which he was sailing to Australia sank with all hands off New Guinea.

Sir John Millais himself received an omen of his own death which he failed to recognize at the time. In order to relax his mind from the constant strain of painting portraits of society women, he would amuse himself in sketching whimsical supernatural studies, humans shadowed by ghosts and the like. He confided to his friend Violet Tweedale (who later reported the matter in her book on psychical experiences) that when he indulged in this weird art, the figures 881896 would appear and disappear repeatedly upon the canvas. He was quite superstitious but would have dismissed this trivial hallucination from his mind had the figures not appeared on so many different occasions.

Mrs. Tweedale did not recognize their significance until the great artist's death. It occurred on August 8, 1896.

THE MONSTER'S FOOTPRINTS *ఈఈఈఈఈఈఈ*

The London *Times* featured the following story in their columns for February 8, 1855:

"Considerable sensation has been evoked in the towns of Topsham, Lympstone, Exmouth, Teighmouth and Dawlish in the South of Devon in consequence of the discovery of a vast number of foot tracks of a most strange and mysterious description.

"It appears that on Thursday night last there was a heavy snow in the neighborhood of Exeter and the South of Devon. On the following morning the inhabitants of the above mentioned towns were surprised at discovering the tracks of some strange and mysterious animal, endowed with the power of ubiquity, as the footprints were seen in all kinds of inaccessible places—on the tops of houses and narrow walls, in gardens and courtyards enclosed by high walls, as well as open fields.

"There was hardly a garden in Lympstone where the footprints were not observed. The track appeared more like a triped than a quadruped, and the steps were generally eight inches in advance of each other. The impressions of the feet closely resembled that of a donkey's shoe and measured from an inch and a half to two inches across. Here and there they appeared as if cloven, but in the generality of the steps the shoe was continuous and from the snow in the center, remaining entire, showing the outer crest of the foot, it must have been convex.

"The amazing creature seems to have approached the

door of several houses and then to have retreated, but no one has been able to discover its standing or resting point.

"At present it remains a mystery, and superstitious people in the district are afraid to go outside at night."

Hundreds of people testified to seeing the spoors in the snow extending over a stretch of nearly one hundred miles of the Devon coast. The most learned investigators looking for trickery could find none. The Ministry of Agriculture declared that the animal was a land mammal and not a sea monster.

It was never learned how the creature was able to leave its footprints in various places without a track leading from one to the other. To this day the people in the district fear another visitation.

THE LITTLE PEOPLE OF IRELAND &&&&

In Ireland and the Highlands of Scotland there are so many rumors about fairies and leprechauns that a group of people have formed the *Faery Investigation Society*, prompted by the deceased poet who wrote, "I think the faery world exists as we exist and some day it will be proved."

Unexplained disappearances, sudden death, and other inexplicable mysteries are accounted for in Ireland and Scotland by the agency of faeries. A story still current in the Isle of Skye about the Macleods of Macleod who own the fine and warlike Castle of Dunraven tells of one of the clan's chieftains who took a faery wife. After a time Lady Macleod received a call to return to her people; when it came she was in the wood close to the castle grounds. As she vanished she dropped a silken scarf which is still preserved by the family and is known as the Faery Flag of Dunraven.

Genealogical records of the Macleods reveal that there actually was one Lady Macleod whose death was never recorded while merely a laconic reference is made to her "disappearance."

Not long ago the *Irish Times* reported a meeting of the West Meath Board of Health in which there was a letter read from a certain Matt Dougherty of Killucan complaining that the faeries had become an intolerable nuisance to him and asking for public protection from their intrusions. "I want you to take my cottage to another piece of land," he pleaded to the Board. "The Little People are displeased, and the life is frightened out of my wife. Whenever she goes to the well for water she sees a little man with a green cap, and he laughs and jeers at her."

Dr. Douglas Hyde, formerly President of Eire and giant of the intellect, claims to have come across a leprechaun when gathering berries some years ago under a shelving rock. It was about the size of a doll, perfectly formed, had a quaintly shaped head with large batlike ears, a sweet little mouth and bright brown eyes.

Other witnesses who have been privileged to see leprechauns, testify that they are about two feet tall, that they have hard, hairy faces like ordinary men. They are usually clad in red clothing with knee breeches and look very much like human beings seen through the wrong end of a telescope.

Watching for faeries is still a popular pastime in Eire. At dusk crowds are sometimes seen congregating at crossroads in the hope of catching a glimpse of them.

As for poor Matt Dougherty of Killucan, the *Irish Times* go on to say that he acutally held one of the annoying faeries in his hands for a few moments. Asked what he wanted, the little fellow said: "It's all equal to you what my business is," and forthwith wriggled loose.

DRACU 🐟🐟🐟🐟🐟🐟🐟🐟🐟🐟🐟🐟🐟🐟🐟🐟🐟🐟🐟🐟🐟

Elenore Zugun was born in 1913 of peasant stock at Talpa, Rumania. From the time of her twelfth birthday, curious manifestations have occurred wherever she happened to be. So, quite often, windows are mysteriously broken by stones that fall at her feet, although no one has ever been seen to throw them.

More mysterious, however, is a very odd manifestation to which her person has been subjected. While washing dishes or doing some laundry, the young woman would often let out a sudden piercing yell and simultaneously an ugly red weal would appear on her thigh or back. There were at times several weals, as though from a severe whipping, and

119

on rare occasions there were teeth-marks in her flesh which looked as if they came from a human bite.

The local peasants feared her and declared that she was a victim of "Dracu." According to them, this demon was responsible for the beatings, and the unfortunate girl became so obsessed by the idea that it became finally necessary to send her to an insane asylum.

There she might have stayed for the rest of her natural life, had not a kind-hearted Austrian woman heard about her and taken a personal interest in her fate. Countess Wassilko-Serechi obtained her release and took her to Vienna where she was given exhaustive psychiatric tests by the well-known specialist, Dr. Karl Weiss.

Meanwhile Baron Schrenck-Notzing, another famous doctor, had begun investigating Elenore Zugun's case. He reported that before the whippings, he and other witnesses distinctly heard a toneless, breathy voice uttering obscene words in Rumanian, followed by faint but sharp cracks of a whip. Examination of the girl's body afterwards would always reveal one or more inflamed welts. On the occasions when there was no voice or sound and the girl recoiled in pain, markings would appear in the form of heavy red depressions, as though she had been bitten quite viciously.

Dr. Weiss was less sensational in his diagnosis and thought that the girl's early fears of "Dracu" possessed her to the extent that the punishments, to which the peasants believe certain people are susceptible, actually appeared on her body due to autosuggestion. He did not venture any theory about the stone-throwing.

MODERN EXORCISM 👹👹👹👹👹👹👹👹👹👹👹👹👹👹

Possession by demons was once the theory for all insanity and all cases were treated by exorcism. The possessed was bound hand and foot in a chair, then given nauseous drugs called "holy potions." These produced moaning and faintness which were regarded as proof that the devil was losing control and was about to be driven from the body. By the side of the tortured victim the exorcist would stand reciting passages from the *Liber Sacerdotalis* or the *Rituale Romanum*.

This process was often continued for hours, and if the lunatic kept quiet and showed no distress, that was taken to mean that the devil, or whoever it was, remained unmoved. Then more drastic "remedies" would follow. Burning brimstone, for instance, would be held to the patient's nostrils, which produced contortions, screams, and fainting spells. No wonder the exorcist's chair was dreaded worse than insanity itself.

There is today a psychiatrist in New York who for years quietly has been treating certain cases of insanity with the aid of trance mediums whom he uses to plead with the possessing demons to withdraw into their ethereal world. Needless to say, the parallel between this method and that of the medieval exorcist does not apply to the remedies used. The modern treatment involves no more discomfort for the patient than, let us say, the therapeutic devices of psychoanalysis.

Dr. Titus Bull is a physician with a distinguished career. He is Research Director of the *James J. Hyslop Foundation for the Treatment of Cases of Obsession* and a member of the *Association for the Advancement of Science.*

His method of treatment is based on the theory that, just as a man's body is the host to innumerable germs, so his spirit may be infested with all sorts of non-physical entities which it would seem to be quite all right to call demons. Their way of operating is apparently not much different from the way a human hypnotist acts upon his subject.

Dr. Bull always examines his cases for physical symptoms first, and spirit intercession is only resorted to after every known and normal form of therapy has been tried. Cases of arrested mental growth as well as brain diseases with organic symptoms do not come within the orbit of exorcism.

A possessing demon is defined by Dr. Bull as the spirit or ghost of an underdeveloped individual, that is, in most cases, an individual who has not controlled his passions and appetites during life and thus could not leave them behind him when he died. By invading a living personality the demon continues to suffer the same cravings and seeks to gratify them vicariously. Through his victim he derives a certain satisfaction not unlike physical sensation.

While the *Foundation for the Treatment of Cases of Obsession* has been almost one hundred per cent successful in its cures, it must be pointed out that the cases of insanity treated in this extraordinary way have not been very numerous. Intercession is slow and the treatment takes a long time. Of the patients cured in a year's work, three had been in institutions for the insane and one had needed to be re-strained by means of a strait jacket.

A particularly striking case is that of a woman who had spent years in an asylum and was considered absolutely in-curable. Today she is leading a useful and normal life again. The onset of her condition came one day when she lapsed into a man's personality and began to pour out the most hor-rible obscenities and bitter blasphemies. After a life of virtue and charitable interest in others she became susceptible to many temptations and would account for it all in statements like these: "The demon is dictating to me all the time. It says: 'You can use your own mind if I let you, but I'm not going to. You were a fool to let me get into your head, but now I am here, I am going to stay. Go on, get mad! Kill yourself if you want to. You can't hurt me; you would only please me. I have control of every nerve and fibre in your body!' "

In the treatment of cases of this sort, Dr. Bull's medium, a Mrs. Duke who is a schoolteacher in a New York Public School, goes into trance and through her he quietly pleads with the demon to leave the patient's mind. In this procedure the medium assumes temporarily the personality of the pos-sessing power. In several cases it transpired that the demon was unaware that he was causing bodily harm to the patient, and Dr. Bull could induce him to withdraw by simply im-pressing upon him the fact that in harming the patient he was also harming himself.

Thus modern exorcism holds out new hope to a group of lunatics who formerly had none.

THE MAN WHO DIED ALIVE ✄✄✄✄✄✄✄✄

Robert Louis Stevenson died in the Samoan Islands in 1894, having suffered from ill health for many years. Two years earlier, in July 1892, Chief Tusitala, as the natives called the author of *Dr. Jekyl and Mr. Hyde*, had a psychical experience which resulted from a normally fatal illness and may hence well be considered a sort of vicarious form of death.

By ten o'clock on a hot hazy afternoon he was weaker than usual. Respiration was reduced to mere gasps; his heart was throbbing rather than beating; and the patient felt certain that his life was quickly ebbing away.

Suddenly he became aware of a new form of consciousness separate from and yet not quite superseding his mortal selfhood in the flesh. Gradually this new consciousness became more individual, as though it were absorbing his past ego, and as it gathered clarity, it seemed to become able to exist outside his body which it could contemplate in full detachment and from which it could wander at will in whatever direction it wished through space and time.

Describing this experience to F. W. Myers, the author of *Human Personality and Its Survival*, Stevenson said there were really no words in which he could adequately tell the story. He recollected a sense of soul-emancipation, such as one might feel on a sunny morning after a frightful nightmare. There sang in his ears a sound like a sweet, sad sobbing and a soaring of restful music, through which watered vistas of light pierced, revealing sparkling seas and smiling shores.

All the major events of his past life were mirrored before him in one great jewel of recollection, a condensation of the memory stream flowing with life through time. At this stage he found he had become omnipresent; he could get up and leave his body completely. He watched his wife come to his bedside and run immediately for the doctor. He followed her step by step to the village.

During this interval, loneliness stole over him. A desolate plain loomed before his eyes, low-lying and unlighted, in the center of which there roamed another lonely man calling out as if in search of a companion. Although he saw and heard this, he could not respond, and the only answer the man received was the echo of his own voice. An oppressive silence reigned as he set off on the run, as if seeking silence by flight.

In due course he saw Mrs. Stevenson arrive, and he watched the doctor injecting into the vein of what had been his arm something he afterwards learned was adrenalin. He heard the doctor say: "I'm afraid this is the end." In what he terms "the divine state of the death-meridian line" the great writer was experiencing strange terrors and exaltations in the remnants of his body-bound consciousness, at once grotesque and rapturous. There was no desire to stir himself, not even to move an eyelid. He was dead.

After what seemed an eternity his heart began throbbing again with slow intermittent thumps. He became aware that his mortal consciousness was reviving and drawing back into itself his detached ego. He stepped back into his body, as it were, but in doing so, all the clarity of vision, the unlimited ability to see anything and everything, immediately disappeared.

Rallying enough to speak, he groaned: "It was so wonderful. Why couldn't you let me be?"

OCCULT MENAGERIE ᚕᚕᚕᚕᚕᚕᚕᚕᚕᚕᚕᚕ

Dr. Gustave Geley was a celebrated French Physician who gave up a flourishing practice in order to take up psychical research. He became Director of the *International Metaphysical Institute* of Paris where he studiously investigated psychical phenomena under fraud-proof conditions.

In his book, *Clairvoyance and Materializations*, Dr. Geley reproduces photographs taken during seances with Franek Kluski, whom he called the King of Mediums. This remarkable medium was Polish, a writer and a poet, not a professional medium. He worked with Dr. Geley without pay, and his seances were significant because he was one of the few mediums who have been able to materialize animal forms which growled and ran about, frightening some of the sitters.

Among the distinguished witnesses of the Kluski seances were such people as Camille Flammarion, the world-famous astronomer, and Professor Richet, the noted physiologist and winner of the Nobel Prize for Science. Their signatures bear witness to what actually took place at Mr. Kluski's seances. And very terrifying it must have been.

Flash-light photographs, for instance, were taken of an animal intermediate between man and ape with a high, straight forehead, a strangely human face, hairy long arms and very strong hands. The form was as large as an adult man and made hoarse noises, clicked his tongue as if he wanted something to eat. The creature gave off an acrid scent reminding the sitters of the smell one encounters in a menagerie. Its stature suggested strength sufficient to move heavy objects, and though its behavior caused fear among the audience, it always obeyed Mr. Kluski.

At another seance, Dr. Geley records, Mr. Kluski materialized a rapacious beast the size of a large dog which Professor Richet described as a maneless lion. This animal exhibited quite an emotional nature, running around and licking the hands and feet of the sitters. "It pulled my trouser leg and its cold nose touched my hand," Dr. Richet recalls. "The beast left queer paw-marks wherever it had been."

Photographs were also taken of a huge bird which rose in the air, emitting a terrifying scream and finally vanishing in the same way as human phantoms do.

Zoologists who came to identify these mysterious creatures were unable to do so. Professor Pawlovsky of the Massachusetts Institute of Technology declared them to be of no species known to science. The intermediate animal resembled to some extent, he thought, our conception of the Pithecanthropus.

"However strange these materializations of animals may seem, their reality is not in doubt," Dr. Geley concludes.

SIX

A PHANTOM COMPANION 🏵🏵🏵🏵🏵🏵🏵🏵🏵🏵🏵

In Tibet man is in continual conflict with the elements; he is faced by mountains that brook no crossing; the earth gives little or no food; snow, ice, hail, and burning sun smite his crops; and it is little wonder that implacable demons and fiends seem ever to be seeking his destruction and mock him from the distant snows.

Madame David-Neel, a diminutive, Parisian-born explorer, was the first white woman to enter the Forbidden City of Lhasa and knows a side of Tibetan life which is a sealed book to most explorers. She has spent years in the Land of Eternal Snows, is the friend of hermits who sit for years in mountain caves in the vow of darkness and silence, and has witnessed many of the weird ceremonies for which Tibet is famous.

An example of these is "chod," a mystic banquet and ceremony of initiation for those who want to become lamas. The site chosen is usually a wild, lonely place calculated to increase the eeriness of the proceedings, and the hour is always at dusk.

"A little ballet is performed by ascetics in ritual robes wearing horrible masks," explains Madame David-Neel in one of her books. "These initiates become so stimulated in their imagination that they actually believe they are preparing themselves to be devoured by demons.

"The celebrant must concentrate on a feminine deity that stands before him with a bloody sword in her emaciated hands and in one fell swoop cuts off the heads of the dancers. Cohorts of ghouls then crowd near for the feast. The goddess severs their limbs, opens up their bellies and devours them.

"When the mental torture has become unbearable, the novice is permitted to let the demonic vision of the banquet vanish. Gradually the hideous laughter of the ghouls fades away and the initiate must imagine that he himself has become a mass of charred bones."

The climax of Madame David-Neel's Tibetan career was reached when she learned to create actual material forms in the image of her thought by sheer power of concentration. The pert little Frenchwoman had become lonely in the solitude of a mountain retreat and she decided to carry out the secret formula, for she knew that a successful thought-form appears to its creator, as well as to others, as an objective human being.

"I chose for my experiment," she told one of her friends," a most insignificant character—a man that would be quite safe—short and fat, of an innocent and jolly type." And verily, after a few months, Madame David-Neel's man was finished, his bulky figure growing gradually life-like and usable.

"For a time he did various chores for me but then I found him doing things that I did not command. He would stop and look around when I was undressing. I would sometimes feel his robe brushing against me."

Then an awful thing happened. The man began to alter. Before her very eyes he slowly changed into a lean and evil-looking fellow.

On one occasion a herdsman delivering milk saw the phantom and took immediate flight, informing the district about his experience so that the little woman and her phantom companion became totally isolated.

It took Madame David-Neel about six months to dissolve the man with the help of the formula the hermits had taught her, so tenacious of life was he.

THE REVENANT MODEL 🪰🪰🪰🪰🪰🪰🪰🪰🪰🪰🪰

Gerald Brockhurst, the distinguished British artist now living in the United States, is widely known for his portraits of the Duchess of Windsor, General "Hap" Arnold, and Bernard Baruch. A remarkable quality of his work is the perfect likeness which he succeeds in capturing from his sitters, and his early efforts were greatly aided by the facility with which he could accomplish the finished portrait if need be with only one sitting. Busy people were glad to be spared the tedious sittings required by other artists, and Brockhurst's products succeeded in being every way as good as theirs.

Brockhurst is of course aided in his accomplishments by a remarkable visual memory and absolute mastery of the techniques of portraiture, but long ago he discovered that certain people—as he likes to describe it—leave behind them an etheric double which can be called upon to pose at any time convenient for the artist and wherever the prototype may happen to be.

The method which Brockhurst uses seems natural enough. He looks at his sitters most attentively, sketching from time to time on the canvas but really fixing in his mind's eye the features so indelibly that they become enshrined in his memory. Then he puts the canvas away and begins another sitter.

Later on he locates the "etheric double," seats it in a chair, and proceeds to paint it just as if the sitter were before him in person. The extraordinary thing now is that the double often appears more vividly than the person in the flesh so that the artist is able to get a better likeness from it than from the sitter himself.

Quite a few years ago, Brockhurst was staying in the picturesque town of Carnac, in Brittany, for the purpose of doing some landscape sketching. He was sitting outside a tavern, having some evening coffee and enjoying the balmy summer air. Moonlight streamed down on the village thoroughfare which was swarming with people. There passed by crowds of tourists and local residents, a conglomeration of well-dressed and for the most part self-sufficient folk.

Suddenly he was struck by the appearance of a young woman. She was really a wisp of a girl, rather slim with a complexion white as milk, set off against very blonde hair and eyebrows; but it was her downcast expression that attracted his notice most particularly. She wore a kerchief round her head which seemed to accentuate her pathetic mood, and she reminded Mr. Brockhurst of one of the tragic heroines of Maeterlinck's plays. The color of her eyes he could not see for she passed by with determined steps, signifying that she was bound on some important errand.

A few nights later, in his hotel room, Brockhurst thought that he would try to coax his eyes to recall the form and lineaments of this strange little girl whose image he could not forget. So he set himself to picture the pale face, the blonde hair, the pose of the head and neck with a view to sketching her. There, he said to himself, her arm would rest on the elbow of the chair, there her dress.

Unexpectedly, as if his efforts at picturing the image had nothing to do with it, the sad vision appeared before his eyes. For some minutes he sat silent, reveling in the possession of his accomplishment, afraid to move lest the beautiful apparition should fade away forever. Although he was aware that this was no ghost but a simple natural illusion, there was something that distinguished it from the usual materializations which he used for his portrait sitters.

The likeness to the original was absolutely perfect, but what amazed his sensitive observations was the fact that the eyes, which he had never seen, blended into the personality as if nature had created them. The image seemed as if it would like to speak and move about, but it remained utterly still.

As Mr. Brockhurst sat entranced he heard footsteps outside and a knock at the door. Opening it he found the proprietor's wife with a telegram for him, and as she handed it through the half-open door, she looked in the direction of the chair where the image was seated, and gave a most perceptible start. Then she took her leave with a suspicious glance at the artist. Was it possible, he asked himself, that his dream picture had become a spatial reality for the eyes of another?

At once the pallor of the girl gave way to an indignant blush, as if she were embarrassed at being found in a man's room unchaperoned. After a few minutes Mr. Brockhurst felt embarrassed, too, and instead of beginning to draw, he dissolved the image and went out for a walk.

Next day he was visited by a local gendarme. In a peremptory manner he asked: "Where is Mlle Leclerc? She has been missing from her home and was seen in this room by the proprietress last night."

Mr. Brockhurst was at a loss as to how to explain his position. Investigations continued for some hours, and fortunately the evidence absolving him was not long in being brought to light. The body of Mlle Leclerc was found at the bottom of a steep and lonely cliff along the coast. She had committed suicide on the night he chose to sketch her.

KILLING BY WILLING (I) 🪶🪶🪶🪶🪶🪶🪶🪶🪶🪶🪶

Two rival medicine men met one noon in the blistering heat of Central Australia. "Die," said one to the other, leveling his forefinger at his face and fixing a pair of fiery eyes upon him. The recipient of this injunction dropped dead instantly, and the witch doctor was arrested. Investigation revealed that the man had died of heart stricture, although the coroner pointed out that he could have died of autosuggestion, that is, in less learned terms, by the strength of his blind faith in supernormal powers. This fantastic occurrence took place in 1945, not in 1645 or 1745!

A short time before, a well-known native named Hector, a magnificent specimen of the aborigines and, incidentally, a local celebrity as the man who ran thirty-seven miles to bring help to some crashed allied fliers during the recent war, died in a similar mysterious way. He was a victim of the dreaded death-pointing bone which can be described as a bow discharging a lethal message instead of poison arrows.

In some way or other this worthy had incurred the displeasure of his tribe. One evening, when he returned rather late to his dwelling, all the muscles of his fine body were trembling like leaves. His breathing was labored and there was the catching in his throat which announces imminent death. "They pointed the bone at me," was all he found strength to say. A white doctor was called in, but modern medicine is usually impotent against "bone magic." In a short time he had shrunk to a shriveled and bent figure, and he had lost the will to live. On his death the autopsy report read laconically: "Cause of death: Obsession and persecution complex."

Even though it is against the law to use the death-bone, the attendant ceremonies are a familiar sight to any explorer who has ever been in the Australian bush. The potencies of the bone seem to be highest at the hour of dusk. It is operated by two tribesmen who normally withdraw with it behind some thicket or copse. There they sit in a crouching position, one of them chanting a harrowing dirge of death while the other manipulates the bone itself. Attached to its end is a tuft of twisted hair which for some reason or other must be pulled against one's right hip. Marked around it there are rings, indicating the length of time the killing will take, and these are burned off as the victim grows correspondingly weaker.

In the Australian bush the death-bone seems to be a fairly popular instrument of murder. Young girls have been known to "bone" men who had spurned them, and women have been heard to boast of the number of people they have done to death in this way.

White doctors who have practiced in countries where black magic holds sway, have listed the symptoms which the application of the death-bone is said to produce. They are: severe mental strain with concomitant fright, oppression anxiety of neurotic intensity, visual hallucinations, and a feeling of impending calamity.

Not long ago the Earl of Errol went to Kenya Colony on a big-game hunting expedition. One day he started out alone on a preliminary scouting tour. As he walked through a piece of jungle where some magic native symbols were displayed, the witch doctor who was using them in the practice of some sort of exorcism remonstrated with him, imploring him to use another path. The earl, who was not familiar with the strange customs of Africa, paid no attention and gaily went his way.

On returning to his quarters Lord Errol complained of not feeling very well. A strange lassitude took hold of him, followed by utter prostration. Since he had never heard of, nor evidently believed in, the deadly potencies of evil thought, he should not have been susceptible to the vengeful ministrations of the native witch doctor, but his symptoms were unmistakable to the white physician who was called to his bedside. The witch doctor was tracked down and when threatened with police action, he agreed to call off his curse. Lord Errol gradually emerged from his stupor but only to be murdered in Kenya Colony in 1940.

KILLING BY WILLING (II) &&&&&&&&&

When Anna Kingsford (1846-1881), a noted authoress and the first prominent anti-vivisectionist, got married, she was living in London with her husband in a suburban street where a certain man with a barrow annoyed her by his crying of goods for sale each Sunday. His constant droning of "shrimps and watercress" so got on her nerves that one morning she said to Mr. Kingsford: "I wish someone would choke that man to death."

Soon afterwards the man's cries were heard no more and she forgot the whole thing until some months later, looking up from his paper, her husband said to her: "Well, your wish has come true. That barrow fellow *is* going to be choked to death. It seems he has been convicted of murdering his wife and has been sentenced to be hanged."

In this way Mrs. Kingsford got the idea that she had the power to will no end of things. By her own claim she was responsible for clearing away numerous frauds and men and women whom she considered public enemies. When the Kingsfords moved to Paris about 1878, she became very much interested in and concerned about the accounts of "cruelties" practiced on animals by the physiologists at the Pasteur Institute.

Seeing in Claude Bernard the foremost living representative and instrument of vivisection, she warned him to end his work or take the consequences. The great physiologist replied with a flippant note which made Mrs. Kingsford invoke all the passion of hatred within her. She willed that he end his experiments with vivisection or die. Actually within less than twenty-four hours Claude Bernard fell prey to a mysterious fever and passed away.

But the work of vivisection went on and Mrs. Kingsford sent another message of warning to the Institute. No response was received and the prominent physiologist Paul Bert died shortly afterwards, the second victim of Mrs. Kingsford.

Still the men at the Pasteur Institute used animals in their experiments. Mrs. Kingsford now threatened Pasteur himself, but the great-hearted scientist was as defiant as his colleagues. Hurling all the psychic force she could muster on his head, Mrs. Kingsford was pleased to learn that Pasteur, suffering from a rare infection, was at death's door for several months. However, when death finally did make up its mind to strike, it chose Mrs. Kingsford herself and allowed her intended victim to survive her by fourteen years.

THE HUMAN AIRPLANE (I) ✿✿✿✿✿✿✿✿✿

Sir William Crookes, the celebrated physicist, said of Daniel Dunglas Home: "On three separate occasions I have seen him completely raised from the floor. There are, in fact, at least one hundred recorded instances of Home's rising from the floor, in the presence of as many separate persons. The accumulated evidence establishing Mr. Home's levitation is overwhelming."

Had levitation been a crime, this wizard would surely have been convicted. And unlike many of the great magicians of the world, he never sought to make money out of his ability to defy the laws of gravity. He only demonstrated in order to advance occult science.

On the night of Wednesday, December 16, 1868, at number 5 Buckingham Gate, London, he was being entertained by his friend, the Earl of Dunraven. Present also were Lord

Lindsay and Captain C. Wynne among others. After dinner, Home said: "You have all seen me suspended in air under circumstances where there was no danger. I am now going to perform the most remarkable feat of my entire career. I beg you to remain calm and keep your places."

So saying he went to the window and opened it. Then he went into the adjoining room and locked the door from the inside. Soon there came a loud purring sound which told his friends that he was passing into trance. Lord Lindsay winced: "Oh, my God! I believe I know what he is going to do. It is too horrible. He is going to try to float out of the window into this one. Someone must stop him. It is sheer suicide." He rushed to the locked door, shrieking protestations, but it was too late. The noise of the window next door being opened was the only answer.

The little audience shivered as they waited, their eyes staring in rapt attention at the deepening twilight without. Captain Wynne went over to the window to part the curtains as wide as possible in order to admit Home if he succeeded in his undertaking. He felt a creep of horror as he looked down. There was no ledge outside and nothing to offer a footing down to the pavement seventy to eighty feet below.

The flames of the gaslight swayed violently, and gradually there came to be heard a loud humming sound. Then, to the stupefaction of all present, Daniel Home came floating through the window, head first, his body quite rigid but resting on nothing. Limply it slumped into an armchair and Home began coming out of his trance.

Lord Lindsay left behind a sworn affidavit on this occurrence: "Home contrived his amazing levitation without the aid of any mechanical apparatus. Of that I am certain. But I do not pretend to understand the occult power he used."

Home defied his fate by dying in his bed in 1886, taking his secret with him.

THE HUMAN AIRPLANE (II) ✿✿✿✿✿✿✿✿

In the last World War, Saint Joseph of Copertino was proclaimed officially the Patron Saint of Aviation, and not without justice. In his day (1603 to 1663) he was known as the Flying Friar, for he was endowed with the gift of flight without the aid of wings.

There are on record testimonies vouching for his aerial flights by several hundred persons, including Pope Urban VIII and eight cardinals. The Holy Father was so impressed with the feats of Joseph Desa (as he was called originally) that he insisted on swearing out an affidavit which reads as follows:

"Stupendous was the flight Joseph exhibited on the night of Holy Thursday. He suddenly flew towards the altar in a straight line, leaving untouched all ornaments of that structure; and after some time, being called back by the Father-General, he returned flying to the spot from where he set out."

This human aeroplane performed flights also in Naples

and Assisi where his spectators were men of science and rank. While the Lord High Admiral of Castille, an Ambassador of Spain to the Vatican, was passing through Assisi with his wife, he paid a visit to the Church. The two Spaniards were suddenly overwhelmed to see the Friar throw himself into flight, passing over the heads of the congregation in order to embrace the feet of a Madonna high up in the nave.

Detaching himself from the statue, the Ambassador recorded, he went like lightning, gyrating hither and thither about the church.

One of the saint's contemporary biographers, Antonio Chiarello, relates how he was walking with him in a monastery garden one day and, gazing upwards, remarked how beautiful were the heavens. "Whereupon," he says, "Joseph flew upon a tall olive tree and there remained in kneeling posture for the space of half an hour. A marvelous thing it was to see the branch which retained him swaying lightly, as though a bird had alighted upon it."

The Sacred Congregation of Rites in Rome ordered an investigation into the levitations of the Friar and examined several hundred persons who had seen him fly. The conclusion drawn by that body asserted beyond doubt that at times Joseph Desa could defy the laws of gravity. However, he was canonized for his life of abnegation and piety.

In August 1663, he was stricken with a strange illness after a remarkable flight. The doctor who attended him observed that when he applied the cautery, Joseph became raised about one foot from the couch and entered at will into an ecstatic state which deprived him of all feeling.

On Tuesday, September 18 of that year, the spirit of Saint Joseph took flight, leaving behind the body to which it had been harnessed for sixty-one years.

RAIN-MAKING 🦜🦜🦜🦜🦜🦜🦜🦜🦜🦜🦜🦜🦜🦜🦜🦜

The summer of 1923 happened to be one of terrible drought in China, and conditions boded to worsen into a serious famine. All good Chinese were busy invoking rain by entreating intercession from the Iron Rain God, but one day followed another without a cloud moving in the unbroken luster of a sapphire sky.

By a coincidence the Tashi Lama of Tibet, the Spiritual God of his country, was living in exile in Peking, and on account of the remarkable psychic powers attributed to him it was natural that the Chinese authorities appealed to him for help.

The Lama agreed to use his powers at a special ceremony to be held in Central Park, the scene of all important gatherings in Peking. There he appeared before an audience of about ten thousand persons.

Mounting the platform, the Lama drew a circle and stood in the midst thereof. One of his disciples lit some incense and the Great Man bowed his head in silent meditation. He made an impressive tableau in his picturesque dress, surrounded by a little group of his followers. When finally he kneeled to pray, there was still not a cloud in the sky for as far as one could see. He then spoke as follows: "Lord of the World. I swear by Thy great name that I will not remove from the place whereupon I now kneel until Thou hast pity on Thy children and sendest rain."

The few members of the white colony present were wondering how this demigod would be able to extricate himself from what seemed a most embarrassing situation in which nothing less than his whole spiritual reputation and earthly following was at stake.

For a while nothing happened. But at four in the afternoon great clouds began to gather and by a quarter to five there was almost a cloudburst, lasting until seven o'clock that night.

The Spiritual Ruler of Tibet had not only saved thousands of people from starvation, he had also converted many more disciples to believing in his powers.

BEYOND THE FIVE SENSES ✿✿✿✿✿✿✿✿

In March 1943, Dr. J. B. Rhine of Duke University announced through his *Journal of Parapsychology* that he had proved conclusively that there is a part of the mind possessing the power to affect inert matter.

In the experiments which led to this discovery, Dr. Rhine's subjects were asked to "will" that certain numbers of a falling die should come up. A machine threw dice thousands of times onto a table near which the subject sat concentrating on a certain die-face. The results showed incontestably that the mental force had been at work on the dice. The desired number appeared much more frequently than could have been expected according to the laws of chance.

For many years now Dr. Rhine has been investigating scientifically the supernormal forces latent in man, and he has helped enormously in creating a new science which has made such phenomena as precognition, clairvoyance, and thought-transference, an admitted reality. Through the work of his Parapsychology Laboratory at Duke University, extrasensory perception is now accepted as a primary datum of science.

In the first experiments, Dr. Rhine used a special pack of playing cards, and in the tests for precognition the subject tried to predict what the order of the cards would be after the deck was shuffled by machinery. The participant wrote down his prediction, and over a long series of tests produced an average rate of scoring which ruled out pure chance as an explanation.

Then tests were conducted in relation to space and time. The subjects hazarded guesses at the order of the cards ten days ahead of the shuffle, and again statistics showed that enough correct guesses occurred to exclude the chance theory as a satisfactory explanation.

In tests for telepathy, cards were used which bore certain symbols, such as stars, circles, squares, etc., and the percipient tried to pick the images out of the sender's mind.

Distance experiments have been made in which the divinity student Pearce of Duke University set a record. He sat in a room two hundred and fifty yards away from the sender who, every five minutes, timed by a synchronized watch, turned up a card, studying it intently. Pearce named correctly 19 out of 25 symbols, truly a most remarkable score.

Long distance experiments with significant scores have been made from Durham to Los Angeles and more recently even across the ocean. Dr. Karlo Marchesi, a physician at Zagreb, Jugoslavia, a keen student of psychical research, was the percipient in a fascinating experiment involving intercontinental distances.

At 5 P.M. one autumn day in 1947 (10 P.M. Greenwich Mean Time), a deck of special cards was shuffled at Durham, and as individual cards were turned up in five minute intervals, each one was held up in the direction of Zagreb. Dr. Marchesi not only recorded his guesses but also the outdoor barometric readings of the hour. The tests were repeated over a period of time, and it was found that his guesses were more accurate on days of low humidity, implying, perhaps, the existence of a sort of psychic "ether."

Along with the card tests a stimulus picture was also transmitted, some sort of simple drawing, unknown to the doctor in Zagreb, in response to which he attempted to draw the "telepathic impact" of it on his mind. Unfortunately the results of this test were censored in the mails (they did look suspicious!) and a true check was never obtained. However, the verified scores of Dr. Marchesi proved clearly that the mind of man is capable of transcending the space-time limitations of the physical world at a distance of four thousand miles quite as well as through the opacity of a stone wall.

Dr. Rhine's experiments as a whole have established that the faculty of extrasensory perception varies considerably from one person to another. The psychology student Linzmayer of Duke University carried out a series of tests at the Parapsychology Laboratory and one day, in a test for clairvoyance, he made nine correct "guesses" in a row, which was then an all-time record. This subject found that he was more clairvoyant when able to commune with nature and once, when driving with Dr. Rhine in an especially scenic part of North Carolina, he bettered his own record and made fifteen successive correct "guesses."

But the divinity student Pearce topped the record set by Linzmayer. At the end of a thrilling bout of tests with him, Dr. Rhine decided to see what a monetary incentive would do to increase results. After the student had identified twenty cards correctly, the professor said: "I'll bet you a hundred dollars you can't guess the next one right."

Pearce concentrated intensely. His guess was right again. Another bet was proffered and again he named the right card, until he reached a total of twenty-six, establishing a new record which, however, has since been equaled several times.

Dr. Rhine intends to turn his curiosity to research on the supernormal phenomena produced by spiritualism, for he feels that his proof that the mind is independent of the space-time system represents an implied proof of some sort of physical survival beyond the grave.

THOUGHTS ON THE WING 🕭🕭🕭🕭🕭🕭🕭🕭🕭🕭

The night before his departure on the arctic rescue flight in search for some Russian airmen, who were believed to have been forced down near the Bering Strait in October, 1937, Sir Hubert Wilkins, the celebrated explorer and aviator, spent a few hours at the City Club of New York. There he chanced to meet Harold Sherman, an old acquaintance of his, who is known to the general public as the author of several books on mental discipline. Sir Hubert had heard vague rumors about his remarkable telepathic powers, and almost without overture, the conversation drifted toward the fascinating subject which, under the somewhat forbidding name of extrasensory perception, Dr. Rhine had recently brought into the limelight of popular interest.

"It would be great," said Mr. Sherman enthusiastically, "if I could receive impressions from you when you are in the Arctic. Think of what it might mean, if you are forced down and find your radio out of commission."

And so it came about that the great explorer and his friend agreed on an experiment which might be of value in charting those regions of the mind of man which are, to most of us, as mysterious and trackless as the unending wastes of the Arctic. It was arranged between the two men that every night from eleven-thirty to midnight (Sherman's time) each of them was to seek solitude, Sir Hubert concentrating in thought on certain events of the day, impressions of which Mr. Sherman would endeavor to receive telepathically. The impressions were to be carefully written down, and dated copies were to be sent to two impartial witnesses, one of whom was Dr. Gardner Murphy, Professor of Psychology at Columbia University. Whenever possible the text of these depositions was also to be radioed or telegraphed to Sir Hubert in the Arctic.

It was agreed, furthermore, that if Sir Hubert got into difficulties and if his radio became inoperative, he was to concentrate on the figures expressing the latitude and longitude of his location. If either his companion or himself was injured, he was to think of the color red; if his companion was killed he was to think of black . . .

On the afternoon of October 22, Sir Hubert Wilkins, piloted by Air Commodore Hollick-Kenyon, took off from Floyd Bennett Field, New York. The radio of the New York *Times* kept in communication with the rescue plane which arrived after weather delays at Regina, Northwest Canada, on November 11.

Overburdened with the task of organizing the complex details of his incursion into the great white wastes of the Arctic, Sir Hubert failed to keep his appointment with Sherman for the first few days. The percipient sat in his New York room and studiously wrote down his impressions which were sent on to Wilkins by telegram: "You in company men in military attire—some women—you in evening dress."

Sherman himself did not attribute much importance to these preliminary messages the absurdity of which could be excused as being due to faulty tuning-in. For after all, if there is one thing which it is obvious an arctic explorer would not be likely to have with him, it is a tuxedo. But

148

Sir Hubert telegraphed back: "Many officers army and police in uniform for Regina Armistice Ball. My appearance possible through loan of evening dress."

On November 18, Sherman received the thought-form emitted by Sir Hubert with unusual clarity. His return message that day read: "Tomorrow nine thirty A.M. you plan some definite action—perhaps resume flight—something important," to which Sir Hubert replied: "Left word to all members expedition staff be at airport nine A.M. for take-off at nine thirty."

Just as though he were watching the flight personally, Sherman saw almost every detail in his mind's eye. "You following Mackenzie River," he wrote on November 22nd. "Weather fog and snow—down at town with old stone fort —expect flight on tomorrow morning. Aklavik goal." This was confirmed by Sir Hubert's reply: "Followed Mackenzie from Fort Resolution. Aklavik this day. Flew through snow and fog."

Most curious were the rather trivial impressions which came through although the sender had made no special effort to transmit them. So at one time, Mr. Sherman felt very strongly that a dog had been seriously injured at Aklavik and radioed accordingly: "Was injury to dog sustained in fight with others or something falling on it?" Actually Sir Hubert had come upon a dead dog while out walking, and examination showed that the animal had been shot through the head. His mind was naturally preoccupied with this matter, for if dogs are man's best friends anywhere, in the Arctic there are many additional reasons to cherish and almost revere them, and "dog-slaughter," as it were, is there a heinous crime to which one will pay more than passing attention.

On another occasion Sherman seemed to catch a glimpse of a funeral service, and he telegraphed: "Has some citizen of Aklavik died?" Sir Hubert advised him that an Eskimo baby had passed away that very day and that he had attended the funeral.

Suddenly Sherman was alerted from these comparatively unimportant impressions by a very definite flash of red. In response to his solicitude, Sir Hubert wired back: "Radio man sick at Barrow." At about this time Sherman also received the impression of a crackling fire, as though a plane were burning, with a large crowd round it. Fortunately this turned out to be an Eskimo shack which had caught fire and represented no serious loss.

Gradually it became apparent that Sherman was receiving impressions of events before they had occurred. Radio communication became more and more difficult, and Sherman's reliable information became more important as the expedition reached higher latitudes. On January 27, Sherman sent word to Sir Hubert that he had the distinct impression that the searching party would soon make an unsuccessful attempt to take off from one of the stopping places. There would be some troublesome incident occasioning further delay. This came true about ten days later when a mechanical breakdown did cause considerable delay but luckily no serious difficulties.

Soon afterwards the Soviet Government decided to abandon further attempts to find the lost men.

A communication from Sherman to Sir Hubert, dated

March 7, read as follows: "Was tail of plane damaged in bumpy landing? Seem to see some work in rear of plane—fleeting vision of your face—quite strained, intent expression—seems flight started and down at some point or turned back. Snow and sleet pelting on plane. Strange feeling in pit of stomach or solar plexus."

At first blush this message did not make sense to Sir Hubert, but he made a mental note of it in case it might turn out to be a premonitory impression. A few days later the expedition set out fully loaded with 1200 gallons of gasoline, intending to make the long flight back to an Alaskan base. Immediately after they had taken off, it began to snow and sleet with fury. After fifteen minutes in which the ship tossed around like a cork on the ocean, Sir Hubert ordered that they return.

Negotiating a landing was very hazardous in the terrible blizzard, and in doing so the pilot made the best of great difficulties. The plane came down with a terrific thud, narrowly escaping a serious accident but injuring its tail. It was a mean moment for all the occupants, and as the apprehensive look of strain died on the face of Sir Hubert, he remembered Harold Sherman's unconscious forecast of the event.

SEVEN

THE FACES ON THE CATHEDRAL WALL &

Damp within a wall has a way of sometimes manifesting itself in the form of peculiar stains, either because of increasing dampness or the drying out of internal moisture.

Several such stains appeared some time ago on the south aisle of Christchurch Cathedral in Oxford. Eventually it was noticed that they had begun taking on the lineaments of human faces.

Under the Burne-Jones window, donated by the late Dean Liddells in memory of his daughter and son-in-law (the world-renowned artist), there appeared the profile of an elderly man with a crown of curly white hair and an acquiline nose.

Upon closer examination it was found that another face had begun to form, apparently that of a woman, at considerable height in another part of the aisle.

In about a month the features of the first face had matured

152

sufficiently so that it could be identified as the face of Dean Henry George Liddells himself whose grave was only a few yards away in the Close outside. He was buried there in 1898.

The other face turned out to be a famous chorister whose voice had rung through the great edifice for many years. Her grave also was not far away.

Strangely enough the wall where these manifestations took place had taken on a blueish-white appearance, quite distinct from the usual discoloration in other parts of the Cathedral.

Scientists and psychical research experts have examined the faces, and the former have declared that the composition of the stone is not of a type liable to undergo chemical change. They have also satisfied themselves that the portraits have not been embroidered from obscure markings by human hands. Due to public curiosity the Cathedral authorities have conveniently hidden the faces, one by a new altar and the other by a large board.

The explanation proposed by an official of the British Psychical Research Society assumes that the emotional part of the earthly memories of a man of great gifts would naturally linger round the spot where he took pains to erect a memorial to his daughter, and especially amid surroundings he loved.

The Dean having been a great speaker and the chorister a great singer, that is, the personalities of both having been accustomed to pervading the building in the form of dynamic sound, the effects of their presence would last longer than those of others. It is interesting to note that the Dean's expression, formerly one of austerity, has been replaced by gentleness and benignity.

A similar manifestation was reported many years before this in the South Wales *Echo and Evening Express* for October, 1898, in which the face of Dean Vaughan, once attached to the staff of Llandaff Cathedral, formed from a stain that appeared on the left-hand side of the main entrance. The stain appeared shortly after the Dean's death and grew steadily until it had produced a striking likeness. Authorities declared that they were convinced no human agency was responsible, and the stain eventually dried back as mysteriously as it had formed. It remains to be seen whether the face of Dean Liddells will do the same.

THE HAUNTED MUMMY ఈఈఈఈఈఈఈఈఈఈఈ

A British diplomatist named Douglas Murray, when stationed at Cairo sometime in the seventies of the past century, purchased a mummy as a souvenir to take home. He and a colleague sailed for England, their mummy stowed away with the rest of their baggage.

The first part of the trip was covered without anything unusual happening. But as they were nearing port late one afternoon, the colleague heard a shot ring out from the cabin they were sharing. He rushed there to find Douglas

Murray lying on the floor dead from a self-inflicted bullet wound.

The mummy, packed and labeled for transit, was not thought to be connected with this accident and was presumably delivered to the destination previously arranged.

In 1885, Madame Blavatsky, the founder of the Theosophical Society, was staying with some friends for the weekend at Streatham, a London suburb which was quite fashionable at the time. The moment she entered the house, she began complaining of some malevolent influence. Her host paid little attention, knowing that as an occultist she was inclined to be rather erratic.

After a few hours, however, she declared that the influence was so sinister that she could remain no longer unless something was done to track down the Thing which she found so disturbing. Her host agreed to make a search if she would undertake to direct it.

All through the house she went but nothing did she find until she came to the attic. There, in a musty sort of case long since unopened, her psychic sense directed her to the very same mummy which had been brought to England along with the corpse of Douglas Murray.

Still she felt impelled to leave the house, reiterating her fear that the influence of the mummy was very evil. Before leaving she implored her host to dispose of it at the earliest possible moment.

There was no better person to consult in this matter than the late Sir E. A. Wallis Budge, Curator of Mummies at the British Museum. No man knew more of the forbidden secrets of the East, and he was considered the greatest authority on Old Egypt and Chaldea. He examined the specimen and declared that it was all that was left of the priestess Amen-Rha.

Sir Wallis willingly accepted the mummy as a gift to the Museum, even after having been advised of Madame Blavatsky's warning. In his work, he insisted, he had become inured to superstitions.

Orders were accordingly given to a moving company to collect the mummy of the priestess in Streatham and deliver it to the Museum. But as it was being carried up the hundreds of steps to the Department of Mummies, one of the men in charge stumbled and broke his leg. The next day another was reported to have died, although apparently in the best of health.

All this interested the curator, but he still refused to be intimidated. He went on with the routine process to which exhibits are subjected.

The first thing he did was to have the mummy photographed for the records. This was accomplished without incident, but later it appeared that the negative had developed not according to the face of the mummy-case. Instead there appeared the face of a malevolent-looking woman, very much alive.

By this time Sir Wallis was willing to admit that there was something strange about it all and that he was not dealing with the average brand of mummy. So he decided to make a really thorough investigation.

Fortunately the mummy had not been opened by anyone else, and when the bandages were removed, the body was found to be in a remarkable state of preservation.

The face still bore marks of paint and rouge; the hair was dark brown and wavy, inclined to be coarse; the eyebrows were thick and the lashes abundant; the eyes themselves were almost covered by fleshy eyelids; the nose was arched and the lips very sensual.

The teeth were good with the incisors of the upper jaw projecting as was fashionable in the days when the priestess lived. They suggested death at the age of about forty. The whole expression of the face was one of intense evil.

So far there was no clew to the mystery. Another line of investigation was now pursued. The curator began trying to unravel the inscriptions on the mummy-case.

Usually these are merely ritual and formal prayers, but in this instance they turned out to be representations of quite a remarkable nature.

After long research the symbols were translated to mean that the corpse of the priestess, at her funeral, had been subjected to a certain ceremony known as *Ur-hekau*. This ceremony was supposed to bestow on her certain posthumous powers, enabling her spirit to wander on earth at will. It was believed that the rite would give the corpse the ability to think, remember and even talk.

"The haunted mummy," as it became known, was given a place of honor at the Museum and every year people come from far and wide to look for it.

A VICIOUS NECKLACE ๑๑๑๑๑๑๑๑๑๑๑๑๑

In the issue of May, 1931, of the *Zeitschrift für Parapsychologie*, Baroness von Dalwigk tells about a pearl necklace, the property of her sister, Elinor.

The string was once owned by an Indian Raja and has been in the family of Elinor's husband, an Austrian aristocrat, for two hundred and fifty years. During a visit to her sister and brother-in-law at their castle high up in the Tyrol, the baroness asked Elinor whether she still wore the necklace and was told that it now lay in the family safe because each time she had worn the pearls, some years before, she had had, the following night, a terrible dream about an Indian seeking revenge.

This naturally awoke the curiosity of the baroness and she would not let the matter drop until she had another look at the necklace. Upon examination, the pearls were found to be very faded due to not having been worn for so long, and Baroness von Dalwigk persuaded her sister to put them on for a few days so that their luster might return.

Elinor took them with her to Vienna on a return visit to her sister. While they were attending the theater, she suddenly took the arm of the baroness and whispered in a choking voice: "The pearls are moving around my neck as if they were alive!" Her sister was mildly amused and replied flippantly that they were probably homesick for their ancestral oysters. But she thought little of the matter, attributing it to her sister's vivid imagination.

While driving home that evening, Elinor clasped her

throat and made as if to open the door of the moving car to throw herself out. "Now they are trying to throttle me," she screamed. The baroness stopped the car and examined the neck of her terrified sister. The pearls had indeed tied themselves into a double knot, and in doing so had badly abraded the skin. Quickly she tore the pearls from Elinor's neck and placed them in her handkerchief in which she wrapped them and held them tightly in her hand until they reached home. There the two ladies told the story to Baron von Dalwigk who shrugged his shoulders and, putting the pearls in a leather case, locked them up in his safe.

Next morning Elinor complained that she had not slept well and had been disturbed by her usual nightmare subsequent to wearing the necklace. The baron went to the safe in order to withdraw some document and for the sake of curiosity decided to open the necklace case. To his utter amazement the pearls had knotted themselves into a double "fisher knot."

The necklace remained in the safe of the von Dalwigks up to the time of Christmas a year later. By now the string of pearls was famous among the family coterie of friends and as time mellowed the shock, the baroness urged her sister to wear the pearls at a Yuletide reception they were having. It would, she added, be something to talk about for their friends, and after some coaxing Elinor agreed.

At supper the necklace was the subject of scrutiny from all eyes. People had just reached the point when the novelty of seeing the haunted pearls had worn off when Elinor's lips broke loose with an agonized cry, her eyes protruding from their sockets as happens in semi-strangulation.

She was carried upstairs to bed in a fainting condition, and on examination a doctor treated two severe blood-red contusions on her neck. When she came to it was discovered that her hearing was impaired, although only temporarily.

The doctor put the pearls on the table beside the bed, and before the uncorrupted eyes of those present they began coiling like a cobra, standing up in that fashion for at least five seconds and then falling down in a lifeless heap.

No solution to the riddle of the pearls' behavior has ever been advanced, but in an old book on jewelry Baron von Dalwigk found a reference to certain rare types of people upon whose necks pearls have been known to act in a way akin to the unpleasant experiences of his sister-in-law.

PAGANINI'S VIOLIN ✿✿✿✿✿✿✿✿✿✿✿✿✿✿

Everything to do with Nicolò Paganini bears the impress of mystery: his life, his talent, and his death. He died at Nice in May, 1840, in a house where the event is commemorated by a marble plaque which records the fact and says: "His magic tones still vibrate in the soft breeze of Nice." By the same token, wild gossip of a peculiar kind is still rife about him there.

On account of his lack of respect for religion his remains were refused burial by the Church and were kept for about a year in the cellar of a hatter. They resided there until

Paganini's old friend and admirer, the Comte de Cassoles, arranged for them to be buried secretly at a point on the extremity of the Cap St. Hospice, just below the ancient Saracen Round Tower.

The great artist's body rested here for another year when his son, Achellino, decided to transfer it to Genoa, his father's birthplace. However, the coffin was refused permission to land as the ship in which it was transported had sailed from Marseilles where cholera was then raging. From there it underwent further peregrinations until years later it was given the proper religious service at which superstitious people claimed to see devils dancing round the coffin.

Already during his lifetime very strange tales had circulated for years about this mysterious Genoese maestro. The mould of his face gave the imperious look of genius; the eyes were hollow, sunk deep in their sockets, and beetle eyebrows and lashes bristled around them; the nostrils were so dilated as to give a diabolical effect; and his hair hung round his forehead like tired snakes.

In 1810, Paganini was employed by Princess Elisa of Lucca, Napoleon's sister, as director of her private orchestra. But this position was of short duration and he left at the princess's request. The reason she gave was that the virtuoso insisted on playing music distasteful to her, but actually it was on the advice of her physician. It seems that whenever Paganini played his famous Guarnerius violin she would be seized by hysterics and nervous fits. Moreover, she claimed that as he ran up and down the scale she could hear, faintly but distinctly, a weird undertone of human groans, too startling to be imitated by a living voice.

After leaving the employ of the Princess of Lucca, Paganini's fame grew and his career bloomed. He became known as the greatest violinist the world had ever known. The great Rossini is said to have wept like a child on hearing him play for the first time, and with only a few chords from his fiddle, women were known to have swooned, and the most masculine men would react like effeminate youths.

One day a blind man was outside the hall where Paganini was performing. "How many violinists are in that orchestra?" he inquired. On being told that only one man was playing, he retorted: "My blindness has given me very sensitive hearing, and if that is only one man, he is more devil than man."

Paganini's well-known interest in black magic helped spread the report that he had manufactured his violin strings out of the intestines of one of his mistresses, a beautiful woman who had loved him to the point of suicide. As a matter of fact there is a fully authenticated story which would seem to lend substantial support to this ghastly rumor.

Some time early in May, 1840, a gala concert was arranged for Paganini at Nice during which he was scheduled to play an exceedingly difficult piece called *The Witches*, a dirge which called for all the diabolical power he could muster.

The magic bow began producing the melancholy shudders of the witches' dance with consummate skill. Vivid imaginations must have evoked a phantasmagoria of eerie figures on the stage and as his fiddle flew up the harmonies where none had flown before, there slowly arose a sound of something else, an unmistakably human sound generated from the depths of the instrument. It was like a voice trying to say something, mouthing words that sounded the way they do in a dream.

Paganini threw a defiant, half fierce, half laughing glance at his audience. Suddenly, however, his form became enveloped in what seemed like a transparent mist, and there were those who also discerned the clearly defined figure of a woman whose viscera were protruding.

The maestro continued to drive his bow furiously across the chords, but as though his effort had reached an orgiastic pitch, the bow fell out of his hand and in a second there was a thud and the lean form of the violinist was seen to slump to the floor.

When the terrified manager of the theater got to the scene, Paganini lay crumpled in the most unnatural of postures with the catgut of his fiddle wound curiously around his neck.

He died about two weeks later from what was diagnosed as complications arising from pharyngeal phthisis, a condition the onset of which must have begun some months before.

A CURIOUS REPRIEVE   ✢✢✢✢✢✢✢✢✢✢✢✢

Thomas Pierrepont, official hangman of England, retired from his sixty years' tenure of finishing the law in 1945. All his cases have died with the faces of sleepers, calm and un-disfigured, a fact which Mr. Pierrepont attributes to his faculty of "sizing up" the criminal beforehand. A mere *coup d'œil* through a spy-hole in the cell door, he insists, could tell him far more than weights and measures and higher mathematics about how deep the drop should be for a neat and workmanlike job.

Never has there been a hitch in any of Mr. Pierrepont's executions—with one exception, and a very curious one indeed.

John Lee was condemned for murder in February, 1889, at Babbicombe, Devonshire, and Mr. Pierrepont was called upon to perform the last rites. He was careful to test the trap door several times and stretched the noose with heavy weights in order to remove its elasticity.

Often a murderer, who may have refused to confess to a priest, will whisper the truth about his crime to the hang-man, but what a man tells Mr. Pierrepont when he is on the chill brink of death, is kept as a secret between that man and his God. In this respect too the case of John Lee proved to be an exception. Pierrepont had finished adjusting the noose around the neck of his charge with human rapidity and was getting ready to place the black covering over his face, making him blind to this world as he was about to open his eyes on the next, when the man said: "Last night I had a dream that the trap door would not work. Are you sure everything is in order?"

"Yes," answered the executioner. "I have tested it several times."

So saying he went below the scaffold and pulled the lever,

expecting to hear the body fall heavily with a jerk into the pit. But nothing happened!

Hastily he went underneath the gallows and examined the trap door. All was in perfect order. Above he could hear the heavy nervous breathing of the man. Again he pulled the lever, and again nothing happened. A second time he examined the trap and all seemed as it should be. The witnesses standing with strained attention grew restive. For the third time he gripped the lever and pulled, yet the trap did not spring.

The warden of the prison stepped forward. "There is a tradition, I believe, that if the trap door will not work for the third time, the victim should not be hanged. Mr. Pierrepont, unloose John Lee from the scaffold."

This strange case was brought before the House of Lords and a decision was handed down by that body invoking the ancient statute that the sentence should be commuted to one of life imprisonment.

EIGHT

THE THORN OF GLASTONBURY &&&&&

"The White Thorn doth blossom in the deep of winter to speak to men of Christianity, that religion flourishes best in persecution and is strengthened by the seed of the martyrs." Thus wrote a medieval author about the Holy Thorn of Glastonbury.

Legend says that the original tree of Glastonbury was planted by St. Joseph of Arimathea who went to Britain after the Ascension of Our Lord. He planted his staff in the ground as a token that he would stay here until he had completed his mission to establish Christianity.

The staff instantly took root and a hardy tree grew up which for centuries blossomed every Christmas in testimony of the birth of Christ. A fanatical puritan once tried to cut it down for he regarded it as an object of superstition, but before he could finish the job, the axe-head flew off, very properly hitting his leg, and the tree survived for half a century. In Cromwell's time still another attack was made

166

on it, but pious souls had already taken grafts from it and planted them in secret places at Glastonbury.

To Botanists the thorn is known as *Crataegus praecox*, which means "of premature flowering," and it is said to be a sport of a common Mediterranean variety. The Rev. Lionel S. Lewis, who is now vicar of Glastonbury, writes that it flowers in December as well as in May or June and he has known very severe frosts and gales to destroy all signs of buds, in spite of which on Christmas day it invariably shoots through with new blossoms. Last Christmas there was not a blossom on the tree until December 25.

The Chapel of SS. Peter and Paul at Glastonbury is the first Christian Church founded in England. Because the Cathedral at Washington, D. C., is named after it, Stanley Austin, a cousin of the former Poet Laureate, sent a cutting of the thorn to the late Rev. Henry Gates Saterlee, first Bishop of Washington.

Dr. Saterlee planted the sprig in the Close near the Choir Boy's School (now called St. Alban's School), and with a little help from the Department of Agriculture the tree took root.

Faithful to its tradition it has flowered from time to time at Christmas, thus for instance in the years 1918, 1923, 1925, and 1929. When the Duke of Windsor, as Prince of Wales, visited Washington, he was invited to see the thorn. It was in the month of December, and happily the tree had shot through a few blossoms already. These were presented to the Prince. In commemoration of the event he planted a young oak tree bearing a plaque with his name and the date of planting.

The Rev. Lewis of Glastonbury some years ago revived the custom of sending cuttings of the tree to the King and Queen at Christmas and he does not forget the Dowager Queen Mary. For it is believed that whoever touches the Holy Thorn shall always lead a happy and contented life thereafter.

THE BURIED RELIC &&&&&&&&&&&&

At the close of a sultry summer's day in 1907, when the sunlight was slowly fading from the sky, a gathering of exceptional interest took place at Fulham Palace, the residence of the Bishop of London. It consisted of about fifty persons including ministers of various religions, scientists, antiquaries and also the American Ambassador.

The audience was addressed by an American, a tall athletic type of man by the name of Mr. Tudor Pole. He explained that he was the head of the London branch of a large American firm, and up to the time of the incident he was about to relate, he had not been aware of possessing any kind of clairvoyance other than that of being clear-sighted in business.

In a corner of the room where he was speaking, there lay a little case which held a glass vessel of quite unique shape, rather like a Eucharistic chalice, but lower and wider. It was of a greenish-blue color, and from a distance it looked as if the artist who created it had introduced a subtle ornamentation of almost imperceptible silverleaf which shone softly in the lamplight.

Collectors and connoisseurs among those present had examined the vase and declared that they were unable to trace its origin or to identify the period to which it belonged. Some suggested that it might be late Phoenecian while others felt that its archaic dignity pointed rather to the most ancient period of Venetian glass manufacture. All agreed that the mysterious object was a work of grace and beauty.

Mr. Pole proceeded to explain that at the beginning of the year 1902 he was returning home one evening, his brain full of calculations and figures, when suddenly an internal force of an indefinable kind surged up in him emanating from nowhere and holding him enthralled for a very brief period of time. During this interval he received a direct impression that somewhere near the town of Glastonbury (of which he knew only because he had passed through it by train) there lay buried a relic of the most sacred kind. He did not pay much attention to this odd impression, and after a while he forgot all about it.

It was not until the end of 1906 that the impression again flashed through his mind, and this time a distinct voice spoke to him, reminding him more and more strongly that the holy relic near Glastonbury was waiting for his discovery.

The strange impression occurred more often now. It attained its strongest urge in the month of November when he saw at least three times a day with his mind's eye the detailed picture of a spot half a mile distant from Glastonbury Abbey where the relic was buried by a small spring in a pool. It was as though he were dreaming with his eyes wide open, for these impressions always came in the daytime.

Mr. Pole's many occupations prevented him from going himself to the spring to look for the relic and get rid of his obsession. So he sent his sister who thought of the expedition as a pleasant weekend trip and decided to invite two friends to come along with her. The three ladies, to their great surprise, did find the pool and the spring at a place known as Bride's Hill, and under a large stone which had protected it from injury and human observation, the rainbow-colored sacred vessel which had been indicated by the voice in Mr. Pole's mysterious daydreams.

The ladies did not dare to carry away the chalice and concealed it again under the stone. Upon their return they informed Mr. Pole of what had happened and he in turn went at once to see his vicar who was exceedingly interested in the whole affair, and together the two gentlemen went to Glastonbury and fetched the vase.

Word about the discovery reached the Bishop of London who, being somewhat of an antiquarian himself, arranged the meeting of experts at his home.

The evening discussion remained of course inconclusive, but the account of it received quite a play in the London papers. It made an excellent news story even though no one could foresee that the most fascinating part of it was yet to come. Mr. Pole was going over the newspapers after returning home a few evenings later when the maid announced that a certain Dr. Goodchild wished to see him. A rather learned type of man appeared who, looking him straight in the face, said to Mr. Pole: "I have just read of your discovery of the chalice at Glastonbury. It was I who put it in the spring at Bride's Hill several years ago."

He then went on to explain that he had been a professor at a Welsh university from which post he had retired some time ago. Then he unfolded the romantic incidents that led up to his depositing the relic in the spring.

For many years he had been in the habit of passing his summers on the Riviera. In 1885, a friend who knew of his passion for porcelain and glass vases informed him that there was for sale, in a curiosity shop at Bordighera, an antique vase which looked like a very rare type. He went at once to the shop and purchased it for 150 francs.

Dr. Goodchild gave the vase as a gift to his father in England and had almost forgotten about its existence when seventeen years later a curious psychological experience befell him. One day in September, 1902, he was about to leave his home when he fell into a trance in which a strange form appeared to him. The trance was so obfuscated that he did not remember any visual details of the apparition, but the words it had uttered were very intelligible and had been repeated several times. Dr. Goodchild understood that he was somehow in great danger, for the cup he had bought seventeen years earlier at Bordighera was the "Cup of Our Lord" which He had used at the Last Supper; it was to be taken immediately to some holy ground and be hidden there; at a particularly distressful time for the Faith, it would eventually be removed and would be used in some way for the propagation of the faith of Jesus Christ.

Dr. Goodchild complied with the instructions given him and took the chalice to Glastonbury because he could think of no holier spot in all England.

Controversy about the origin of the cup raged for several months. In the end the materialists won out. It was condemned as of comparatively recent manufacture, but the agency that had seen fit to use Dr. Goodchild and Mr. Tudor Pole as its messengers and tools has never been satisfactorily identified.

THE SHROUD OF TURIN 🙐🙐🙐🙐🙐🙐🙐🙐🙐🙐

As hereditary head of the House of Savoy the exiled Prince Humbert, heir presumptive to the Throne of Italy, is officially the owner of a very precious relic known as the Holy Shroud of Turin.

From time to time during the Nineteenth Century this piece of linen cloth, which bears the impression of a human form allegedly exhibiting the actual features of Jesus Christ, was shown to the public.

For centuries the Shroud was alternately accepted as genuine and repudiated as spurious, and at one time it became the subject of a Papal Bull in which it was spoken of as a forged copy of an older original, and it was inferred that the series of brownish stains, which get fainter toward the edges and merge gradually into the light background of the cloth, had been painted by human hands. The known history of the Shroud dates from 1353 when it was discovered hidden in the Church of Lirey in Champagne.

At any rate, the princely owner of this relic treasured it and on May 1, 1898, arranged once again for its exhibition at Turin. Prior to this it had not been on view for over thirty years, a period during which photography had come of age as a rival of portrait painting. It seems natural that the idea of photographing the relic should now have been projected, and from a number of requests the authorities gave permission to Signor Secondo Pia, a leading expert in the new art, to take some exposures with a view to studying the Shroud more carefully. As a matter of fact, he was prompted more by curiosity than by anything else, and he had definitely no notion as to what formidable scientific problems his experiment was going to bring up.

Naturally Signor Pia expected that his photographic plates would merely show some rather shapeless traces representing the lights and shadows on the Shroud in reverse. However, as the development of the first plate proceeded an extraordinary thing happened. To the incredulous eyes of those present there came to view a complete and positive image of an impressively beautiful human face, of the hands and of the limbs, just as if instead of the shroud an earlier negative picture of the body had actually been photographed.

As a technician in photography Signor Pia was quick to see that the shroud carried a negative impression from the bleeding corpse which had lain within it. The photographic impression on the camera plate (being the negative of this negative) was a *positive*, that is to say, it displayed the exact image of the human being, about whose identity it was difficult to remain in doubt.

Here was the face of the Master in all its grandeur and long suffering, the forehead lacerated by thorns and the mouth twisted in agony, yet gentle and beautiful: the beard and the hair were in confusion and clotted with blood.

The amazing discovery was flashed to the world and attracted the attention of many men of science, but, curious to say, the Catholic Hierarchy seemed less interested. Two French professors, Monsieur Vignon and Monsieur Delage, the first a Roman Catholic of unimpeachable reputation and the other an avowed agnostic, lost no time in going to Turin for the purpose of studying the photographs and investigating the scientific implications.

What struck them first was that the wounds on the body were placed quite accurately in accordance with the accepted tradition. But instead of the hands it was the wrists that seemed to have been transfixed. This made perfect sense for obvious reasons of anatomy. Had the nails been driven into the hands they would never have stood the strain, and Monsieur Vignon succeeded in proving that it was the custom in crucifixions to nail the victim through the wrist. All the other wounds were found to be true to the smallest detail, and it was clearly seen that the body had been subjected to a cruel flagellation some hours before death. Bloodmarks were in accordance with the true circulation of the blood, quite unknown at the time when according to the skeptics the Shroud had been painted.

The scientists proved categorically that the image was

not the work of brush and paint or any other human agency but that it was the result of a transmitted impression thrown upon the Shroud by the body laid beneath it. Due to the Jewish custom of impregnating shrouds with aloes and spices, the linen had been transformed by chemical action of body effluvia into a sensitive photographic agent.

What was extraordinary was that the photographic negative of the Shroud resembled the portraits of Christ by da Vinci and others. Christ's image is not to be found in any portrait of his time, which suggests that perhaps the consecrated type of Christ's features has been created by some form of telepathy, operative in the imaginations of the greatest Christian artists.

SANTO CRISTO DE LA AGONÍA &&&&&&

In the little town of Limpias not far from Santander in Spain, there is a church noted throughout the Christian world for a curious event which took place there on March 30, 1919.

This church contains a finely carved crucifix somewhat more than life size. It is known as the Santo Cristo de la Agonía and is placed high above the altar. On that fateful day, during a service being given by two Capuchin Fathers, a little girl became greatly disturbed, and when asked for an explanation, she said that the crucifix had suddenly become alive, that she had seen it move its face and open and close its eyes.

Just as she had finished telling the Fathers her story, one of the adults, a man known for his erring ways, got up and ran out of the church shouting: "He has come back to punish us. I cannot stay here and face that stern eye anymore."

Realizing the possible danger if this beginning should spread into an epidemic of hallucinations, one of the Fathers spoke to the congregation: "Do not be alarmed, my children. Our Lord can certainly manifest His presence in remarkable ways, but it is possible that in our case we have to do merely with a figment of that poor man's imagination."

All eyes were now focused on the Saviour's image. Another worshiper, this time a woman, cried out: "I can see drops of blood running down the temples. The Holy Face is writhing in agony. His body is covered in sweat."

Then others declared they could see the same thing. By this time the Fathers themselves decided to examine the crucifix. Reverently they crossed themselves and looked up at it. In a trice they turned toward the congregation and one of them said gravely: "What has been stated is true. I have just seen the gaze of the Holy Face pass over the assembly in a gesture of benediction." A scene of intense religious emotion followed.

A pilgrimage to Limpias began and during Holy Week thousands of all classes flocked to the church and witnessed the phenomena. Many made depositions and swore before the Sacred Host that they had distinctly seen real blood oozing from the wounds, and there were some who declared they had seen the face of Jesus give a deep submissive sigh. Not a few of the statements bear obviously the stamp of ecstatic reverie but there is a large residuum of perfectly sober reports by people of education with no possible motive for exaggeration.

The King of Spain sent one of his personal physicians to investigate the matter. This man, a Dr. Maximilian Ortz, went with a very skeptical mind, determined to prove that the phenomena were not genuine.

Standing in the middle of the nave, a few yards from the sanctuary, he saw through binoculars blood trickling from the right eye down the cheek. Here was no wooden image, but a veritable heavenly vision. The doctor was not a little worried by what he had seen and he admitted in his report that he was quite humiliated to witness something so averse to scientific dogma. He rested for a while, and shifting his position turned to look again, confident that he had previously been the victim of an hallucination. But no. The blood was still gleaming on the cheek and trickling on. Still somewhat skeptical, he compared the blood painted on the image by the artist. While that was almost black with age the other was crimson, imbued with movement and life. Moreover, he observed the hair to be glistening with moisture and the body covered with perspiration.

Late one evening when the church was empty, two pious sisters climbed up and took samples of the blood and the sweat which were later examined by chemists and found to be of a human type.

An ecclesiastical commission was finally appointed to make a thorough inquiry, but it seems that the results were inconclusive.

THERESE OF KONNERSREUTH ɷɷɷɷɷɷ

On April 9, 1948, Therese Neumann completed her fiftieth year. For several decades now, Eastertide had invariably been marked in her life by a series of mysterious happenings to her person which today are reflected by lines of pain on her face, adding to her remarkable saintlike expression.

As a child Therese was very devout, being obsessed with the idea that she was on earth for a mission requiring that she accept as much suffering in behalf of humanity as she possibly could. Very early she became a follower of St. Teresa of Lisieux, living the same life of abnegation as the Little Flower.

Due to an accident at the age of twenty, paralysis of the spine set in, together with complications, and later her eyesight failed. All during these dark days, she would pray for the intercession of St. Teresa to restore her to health so that she could carry on her mission.

On May 17, 1924, the date of the canonization of the saint, her father, who is a tailor in the town of Konnersreuth in Germany, entered her room and observed that she was speaking to someone invisible to him. Her eyes were wide open and her face was beaming with beatitude. To his blissful amazement, he saw her get up and walk with great difficulty to the window. On September 30 of that year, her eyesight was restored and the doctors pronounced her completely cured.

From thence forward, once every year, beginning on Good Friday, wounds have opened on her forehead, face, hands, feet, and neck in approximately the same form as those which Christ endured in His Crucifixion. Seven of them appear on her forehead, marking the Crown of Thorns; a gaping hole is struck through each of her feet and hands; and others open at each of the parts where Jesus was injured.

This ordeal is accompanied by visions and ecstasy, lasting about ten minutes, during which she perceives the torments of Christ on the Cross, beginning with a vision of Him on the Mount of Olives, followed by the placing of the Crown of Thorns upon His head and the Cross on His back.

Most interesting is the fact that she utters in pure Aramaic, the language which Jesus usually used, all the words spoken by the Master, and does so in perfect phonetical pronunciation.

Experts in oriental languages have been permitted to listen to her at close range and have declared that her knowledge of this extinct language far surpasses their own. Professors Weseley, Wutz and Punder, all learned men who have devoted a lifetime of study to Aramaic, have been amazed to hear Therese enunciate each word with impeccable accuracy.

Just once the professors thought they had caught Therese making a mistake. When she came to the last gasp, when Christ said: "I thirst," she cried out "As-che," and all the professors thought this should be "Sa-che-na." On careful research it was found that Therese was right; by reconstruction of the dead language this was determined to be the proper expression.

For the duration of her ecstatic vision Therese loses five or six pounds of weight which she regains the moment she comes to.

Many thousands of people have seen Therese in her stigmatic condition, among them scientists and doctors who have examined her and declared their bewilderment at the enigma. So much morbid interest was evinced that in 1927 the Bishop of Regensburg issued an edict forbidding visitors to her home without special permission from him.

At this time Therese Neumann is in good health except for a permanent injury to her feet caused by recurrent wounds which make walking difficult.